A Handbook of Bilingual Education

REVISED EDITION

Muriel R. Saville
and
Rudolph C. Troike

St. Joseph's College Library
Brentwood, New York

Teachers of English to Speakers of Other Languages
*A Professional Organization for Those Concerned with the Teaching of
English as a Second or Foreign Language
and of Standard English as a Second Dialect*

WASHINGTON, D.C.

Copyright 1971
Teachers of English to Speakers of Other Languages
Washington, D.C.
Library of Congress Catalog Card No. 71-155824

2nd Printing, 1973
3rd Printing, 1974
4th Printing, 1975
5th Printing, 1975

FOREWORD

This Handbook has been commissioned by the ERIC Clearinghouse for Linguistics in answer to the growing demand for materials in the field of bilingualism. If bilingual education is to achieve its objectives efficiently and in the shortest possible time, it must lean heavily on linguistics to supply insights in the area of language acquisition and behavior. Both authors, Muriel Saville and Rudolph Troike, are eminently qualified for this task by their training, experience, and professional interest. Since it first appeared, in the spring of 1970, A Handbook of Bilingual Education has been used as training material by many institutions concerned with bilingual education and has become one of the most popular documents commissioned by the Clearinghouse. I hope that all educators concerned with bilingual education will find something here which they can utilize to their own, their students', and ultimately, their country's advantage.

> A. Hood Roberts, Director
> ERIC Clearinghouse for Linguistics

The present edition of the Handbook has been revised by the authors and published by TESOL—in more permanent form than the original—in order to permit the widest possible distribution to teachers and administrators for whom it was originally intended. We are grateful to the ERIC Clearinghouse for Linguistics for its continuing cooperation in making important documents such as this available to the ESOL profession.

> James E. Alatis
> Executive Secretary-Treasurer
> TESOL
> February 12, 1971

CONTENTS

Preface   vii

I. INTRODUCTION
- Statement of the problem   1
- Historical perspective   2
- Some basic questions   3
- Some fundamental considerations   5
- Definition of terms   6
- Selected bibliography   8

II. RATIONALE
- Linguistic factors   10
- Psychological factors   15
- Social and cultural factors   19
- Selected bibliography   22

III. DESIGN   24
- Selected bibliography   32

IV. THE LANGUAGES OF INSTRUCTION
- Phonology   34
- Grammar   41
- Lexicon   45
- Selected bibliography   47

V. PEDAGOGICAL CONSIDERATIONS
- Introduction   49
- The curriculum   50
- Language teaching   51
- Practical teaching suggestions   53
  - Phonology   55
  - Syntax   59
  - Vocabulary   62
  - Reading   63
- Selected bibliography   64

VI. EVALUATION	65
Language tests	66
Home conditions	68
Intelligence tests	70
Testing hints	70
Selected bibliography	71

PREFACE

　This handbook has been prepared to review some of the considerations which are of importance for teachers and administrators involved in bilingual education programs in the United States. It is intended to be of practical value to educators, and to answer specific questions which are relevant for those undertaking a bilingual program for the first time. The theoretical factors introduced from linguistics, psychology, and other fields are selected for their immediate relevance to teaching. The view presented from these disciplines may seem to specialists grossly oversimplified to meet this purpose. The specialist knows that there is much research yet to be done in such areas as first and second language acquisition and varied styles of learning. But the education of children will not wait for definitive answers, and teachers have more need for specific suggestions from linguists and psychologists than they do for an enumeration of all their uncertainties.　At the same time, both teachers and administrators need to be aware of the limitations of our present knowledge in these crucial areas, and indeed may contribute to the accumulation of information. Many of these answers and suggestions are offered with full knowledge that they may change with additional information and experience. It is hoped, however, that this handbook will fill an immediate need in education, and that educators will be prepared to adapt instructional content and methods as new findings on language and learning become available.

CHAPTER I

INTRODUCTION

Statement of the problem

Thousands of children each year first encounter English as a foreign language when they enroll in school, even within the United States. We do not live in a "melting pot," but in a country where different languages and different attitudes and beliefs have coexisted for centuries. The older educational idea that only English should be used as a medium of instruction in the United States has left thousands of children illiterate in their native language, and fostered low achievement levels in English itself. If the goals of education are to be realized with these children of non-English speaking background, the English-dominant educational system must learn to accept their existing linguistic and cultural patterns as strengths to build upon, rather than as handicaps to successful learning.

A child does not begin learning when he comes to school. Education begins in infancy, and much of the sound system and grammatical structure of the child's native language has been mastered by the time he is five years old. His language is rooted in and reflects a set of values tied to a particular group. It is already related to a way of feeling and thinking and acting.

An axiom of bilingual education is that the best medium for teaching is the mother tongue of the student. The use of the native language for classroom instruction allows the education of the child to continue uninterruptedly from home to school, permitting immediate progress in concept building rather than postponing development until a new language has been acquired. There has been some resistance to this philosophy, particularly by those who feel that speaking another language may somehow hinder progress in English. Recent experience in many places proves, however, that an equal or better command of the second language is achieved if school begins with the native language as the medium of instruction and introduces the second language gradually. Furthermore, psychological studies such as that conducted by Peal and Lambert (1962) show that when groups of bilingual and monolingual children are matched for the socioeconomic status of their parents, the bilinguals perform at least as well on IQ tests and have the added advantage of knowing a second language.

Some of the resistance to bilingual education comes from bilingual teachers, who are probably the products of monolingual English school systems. They are successful products, and may feel that children now in school should follow their model. In addition, innovative programs are expensive and demanding—not the "easy" way for teachers or administrators. Also discouraging to new bilingual programs may be the present inadequacy of personnel, materials, or understanding.

But past methods in monolingual English education have often proved ineffective with children who speak other languages natively, and more and more of these children are beginning school every year. For them, learning to read in English may be frustrating if they lack the oral language readiness for it. On the other hand, when a child is ready to read his native language and is not taught to do so, the school misses a valuable opportunity.

A child who starts off with frustration or failure may never catch up. A low self-image, lack of motivation, and unsatisfactory performance are often interrelated handicaps to a child whose initial instruction is in a foreign language—indeed, to any child. These may be compounded by a low expectation of learning capacity on the part of the child himself, his parents, teachers and administrators.[1] There are still some who feel that when a child cannot speak English the first day of school, he "doesn't have any language at all." By failing to recognize the child's native linguistic resources, we prevent him from progressing as rapidly as his experiences and intellectual development will allow. Children will not wait for us to develop ideal educational systems; we have an obligation to do the best we can for them now, in the light of our present knowledge, capacity and experience. At the same time, carefully controlled and responsible experimentation is called for, to advance the state of our knowledge and help determine the best choice of procedures to achieve our educational goals.

Historical perspective

Bilingual education in the United States is not new, but the current high level of interest in it comes after a long period during which the maintenance of any language but English was counter to public policy and popular attitude. The Bilingual Education Act of 1967 has helped

---

[1]Rosenthal and Jacobson (1968) report that the teachers' expectations influence student achievement to a significant degree. Teachers who undervalue students do not provide them with an equal opportunity to learn.

strengthen the growing sense of concern we have for the conservation of our national linguistic resources. Cultural diversity is of recognized value to our national interest, and bilingual programs are fostering increased parental involvement in education and promising enhanced economic mobility for minority groups. In addition, we now realize that bilingualism is not a handicap, but may indeed be a social and academic advantage.

Even before the Bilingual Education Act was conceived, several experimental projects, notably those at Coral Way, Florida, San Antonio, Texas, and at Rough Rock School on the Navajo Reservation were already under way. Many other projects, some stimulated by the passage of the Act, or by the influence of concerned individuals in various localities or bureaus, are now being implemented or are in the planning stages.

As defined by the Act, bilingual education refers to "the use of two languages, one of which is English, as mediums of instruction." This definition is so broad, however, that schools having only one subject-matter course in any language other than English would qualify for inclusion. In terms of the classification of bilingual programs made by A. Bruce Gaarder (1967), most programs in the United States are "one-way" schools, with the native language being added as a "bridge" until the child can move into an all-English program. "Two-way" schools, which give balanced instruction in two languages to all students (e.g. the Coral Way program), are much more common in Europe than they are in this country, but they more nearly approach the ideal of producing students who are truly bilingual—who can function effectively in both English and their native language.

Perhaps the greatest immediate effect of the Act has been to focus attention on the fact that the child who comes to school with a native language other than English does stand in need of special instructional treatment, different in nature from that given to native English speakers. This has resulted in a growing awareness among educators of the important body of theory and method which exists for teaching English as a second language.

The passage of the Bilingual Education Act, then, and the various programs instituted in recent years represent a change in the philosophy of American education, from a rejection of other languages to an acceptance of them as valuable national resources and as valid and even necessary mediums for instruction. The same principles apply to linguistic groups in other countries who do not speak the national language natively, such as Quechua speakers in Peru and Bolivia, or Zapotec speakers in Mexico.

Some basic questions

4 / A HANDBOOK OF BILINGUAL EDUCATION

1. WHAT is bilingual education?

Bilingual education is <u>not</u> just "education for bilinguals," nor is it merely an English as a Second Language program, although ESL is a necessary part. It is an educational program in which two languages are mediums of instruction.

2. WHY have bilingual education?

Some questions of purpose still remain. Is bilingual education a good thing in itself, or is it a compensatory system, just to allow better transfer to English? Goals by most proponents are higher self-concept, academic achievement and socioeconomic level for members of minority groups in the United States, and the understanding and preservation of our collective and diverse national heritage.

3. WHO is bilingual education for?

Bilingual education programs in the United States at present are primarily for children who do not speak English natively. They allow these children to continue their cognitive and linguistic growth in their first language while acquiring English as a second one.

Bilingual education is also for native English-speaking children. It may stimulate their natural linguistic curiosity and help them to realize that there are other equally valid ways besides English for expressing their ideas. But of even more immediate importance, it can help them develop greater understanding and respect for their classmates who speak a different language.

4. WHEN should bilingual education begin?

Young children have an innate capacity for language learning that is greatly reduced when they get older. This capacity suggests that bilingual education will be most successful when it is implemented very early in the school program. Native language habits become fixed by the time a child reaches puberty and are much more likely to interfere with his recognition and production of other languages if he learns them after that age. In addition, an adequate bilingual education program beginning at the kindergarten or first grade level should eliminate the need for later remedial language instruction.

5. HOW does a bilingual education program start?

INTRODUCTION / 5

Programs can be proposed initially by either an individual or a group that recognizes a need for more effective instruction. Cooperation must be present or enlisted between the community and school personnel. Experienced counsel should be sought from such sources as state, regional or national educational agencies and from universities regarding planning and funding possibilities and procedures. In particular, the advice of a linguist experienced in second language teaching should be sought, as one of the most common weaknesses of beginning bilingual programs is that they lack an adequate understanding of the linguistic dimensions of bilingual education. This is only the beginning. Some suggestions will be given below for selection and training of personnel, acquisition or preparation of teaching materials, and other prerequisites to bilingual instruction.

Some fundamental considerations

Perhaps more critically than in any other type of educational enterprise, administrative and pedagogical decisions and procedures in bilingual education need to be based on a sound understanding of the linguistic, social, psychological, and cultural factors affecting students. Although these will be discussed more fully in later sections, some of the most immediately pertinent factors are summarized briefly here.

The linguistic factors which need to be considered are the nature of language, the structures of the native and target languages[2] in a bilingual education program, the student's degree of competence in two language systems, and the way the systems interact. These may be rephrased as a series of questions:

a. What is language?
b. What do educators need to know about the languages of instruction?
c. How do languages get in the way of each other?
d. How can language problems be predicted and preparations made to meet them?
e. How well do the children speak each language?
   How much do they understand?

Psychological factors to be considered are the processes of first and second language acquisition, the problems involved when one individual uses two sets of language skills (the switching process, the sometimes conflicting emotions and attitudes which the speaker as-

---

[2] A glossary of terms which may be unfamiliar follows this section of the handbook.

sociates with his two languages) and the reactions of the bilingual as an individual. These points may be rephrased as follows:

a. How does a child learn his native language?
b. In what ways is learning a second language different?
c. What conditions affect language development?
d. How do attitude and motivation influence learning in two languages?
e. What is the relationship of bilingualism and intelligence?

Sociological and anthropological factors are concerned with the sociocultural settings of bilingualism—the role expectations involved, the social influences on bilingual behavior, and the access which bilingualism allows to two cultures. Significant questions include the following:

a. How does the situation or context affect language use and learning?
b. What influence does the family, community, and peer group have on the bilingual speaker?
c. What are some of the possible repercussions from being bilingual?
d. What different styles of learning might be encountered in groups of bilingual children, and how can these be taken into account in the classroom?

Educational considerations, which must take all of the preceding factors into account, include program design, teaching, and evaluation. Under program design are grouped such factors as program organization and the administrative tasks involved in preparing and implementing a bilingual program. Pedagogical factors include language teaching methodology, language as medium and as subject, scheduling, and the need for motivation and classroom control. Evaluation is concerned with procedures for evaluating the program as a whole, the instructional material, and the achievement of the children.

Definition of terms

A definite agreement on terms is necessary to the success of any communication. Since certain terms used in this handbook and other works on bilingualism may be unfamiliar, or used with unfamiliar meanings, a short glossary of significant terms is included here for easy reference.

articulation—the production of differing speech sounds by altering the shape and size of air passages in the vocal tract
balanced bilingual—an individual who is equally skilled in the use of two languages

bilingualism—the use of two or more languages by an individual

compound bilingual—an individual who translates from one language to the other (usually because he learned his second language under those circumstances), does not keep language systems separate, and experiences considerable interference between them

content words—primarily nouns, adjectives, verbs, and adverbs, i.e. words which have a "dictionary meaning"; contrasted with function words (q.v.)

coordinate bilingual—an individual who has two separate language systems, usually learned under different conditions, which cause minimal interference with each other

degree of bilingualism—how well an individual knows the languages he uses

dialect—the variety of language spoken by members of a single speech community, either regional or social

diglossia—a situation in which each language is typically used in, and considered appropriate to, different types of situations (e.g., home vs. outside, discussing particular topics, in certain roles, etc.)

first language (native language)—the first language learned by a child, usually the language of his home

function words—words used to signal grammatical relationship (e.g., prepositions, articles, and auxiliaries)

idiolect—the unique speech of any individual

interference—how one of a bilingual's languages influences his use of the other—the use of nonnative sounds, constructions, or word-choices as a result of influence from the native language

lexicon—the vocabulary or words of the language

morpheme—the smallest recurring unit in a language which carries meaning (e.g., cat is one morpheme; cats contains two morphemes —cat plus the -s which means plural)

morphology—the study of the structure of words

phoneme—the smallest unit of sound which makes a difference in meaning in a language (e.g., /t/ and /d/ are phonemes of English because they make a difference in meaning in such combinations as tin:din and not: nod

phonology—the sound system of language

phonotactics—the pattern of distribution of sounds in a language (e.g., English /ŋ/ does not occur at the beginning of words nor /h/ at the end

second language—a language learned subsequent to a speaker's native language, sometimes the language of school or of the wider community

syntax—the way words (or morphemes) are related to each other in a sentence—their arrangement

target language—the language which is to be taught

voiced sound—a sound produced with vibration of the vocal chords
voiceless sound—a sound produced without vibrations of the vocal chords

SELECTED BIBLIOGRAPHY

Aarons, Alfred C., Barbara Y. Gordon, and William A. Stewart, eds. 1969. Linguistic-cultural differences and American education. Florida FL Reporter VII, 1.

Alatis, James E., ed. 1970. Bilingualism and language contact: anthropological, linguistic, psychological, and sociological aspects. Monograph series on languages and linguistics 23. Georgetown University Press.

Andersson, Theodore and Mildred Boyer. 1970. Bilingual schooling in the United States. Austin, Texas, Southwest Educational Development Laboratory. (For sale by the Superintendent of Documents, U.S. Government Printing Office, Washington, D.C. 20402. Six dollars per set of two volumes.)

Burns, Donald H. 1968. Bilingual education in the Andes of Peru. In Language patterns of developing nations. Joshua A. Fishman, Charles A. Ferguson, and Jyotirindra Das Gupta, eds. New York, John Wiley and Sons, Inc. 403-413.

Gaarder, A. Bruce. 1965. Conserving our linguistic resources. PMLA LXXX, 2B, May: 19-23.

_____. 1965. Teaching the bilingual child: research, development, and policy. The modern language journal XLIX, 3, March: 165-175.

Haugen, Einar. 1964. Bilingualism in the Americas: a bibliography and research guide. University, Alabama, the University of Alabama Press.

Lambert, Wallace. 1970. Some cognitive consequences of following the curricula of the early school grades in a foreign language. In Monograph series on languages and linguistics 23. James E. Alatis, ed. Georgetown Univessity Press. 229-280.

Macnamara, John, ed. 1967. Problems of bilingualism. The journal of social issues XXIII, 2, April: 138.

Mackey, William F. 1965. Bilingualism. Encyclopedia Britannica, III:610-611.

Paulston, Christina Bratt. 1970. Algunas notas sobre la enseñanza bilingüe del idioma en el Peru. América Indigeno: 99-106.

Rojas, Pauline M. 1966. The Miami experience in bilingual education. On teaching English to speakers of other languages: Series II, Carol J. Kreidler, ed. Champaign, Illinois, National Council of Teachers of English. 43-45.

Rosenthal, Robert and Lenore Jacobson. 1968. Pygmalion in the classroom: teacher expectation and pupils' intellectual development. New York, Holt, Rinehart and Winston, Inc.
Rubin, Joan. 1968. Language education in Paraguay. Language patterns of developing nations. Joshua A. Fishman, Charles A. Ferguson, and Jyotirindra Das Gupta, eds. New York, John Wiley and Sons, Inc. 477–488.
Weinreich, Uriel. 1967. Languages in contact. The Hague, Mouton and Co.
Zintz, Miles. 1963. Education across cultures. Dubuque, Iowa, Wm. C. Brown Book Co.

Journals:
  Human organization
  Journal of verbal learning and verbal behavior
  Language learning
  The modern language journal
  TESOL quarterly

CHAPTER II

RATIONALE

Linguistic factors

Language is a highly complex form of symbolic activity, in which such elements as words (e.g., <u>dog</u>), affixes (e.g., <u>un-</u>, <u>-ed</u>), word form (e.g., <u>fill</u> vs. <u>full</u>), stress (e.g., <u>récord</u> vs. <u>recórd</u>; <u>English teacher</u> vs. <u>English téacher</u>), intonation (e.g., <u>They're coming?</u> vs. <u>They're coming.</u>) and word order (<u>house guest</u> vs. <u>guest house</u>) are fused in systematic ways to organize and communicate meaning. Because language is a primary vehicle for learning, a child's facility in language may affect to a great extent his acquisition of knowledge, his role in society, and his ability to respond to opportunities. It is vitally important, therefore, for anyone engaged in any aspect of bilingual education to possess some basic understanding of the nature of language.

Before dealing with these aspects in detail, we need to consider some fundamental facts about language. Each individual, as a result of his unique linguistic experiences, speaks a slightly differentiated form of the language, which linguists call an <u>idiolect</u>. As a result of parental and peer influences in the course of growing up, the idiolects of people who have been in frequent communication since childhood will tend to be very similar, and will differ from the idiolects of persons in other inter-communicating groups. Any group of similar idiolects differing from other comparable groups in features of pronunciation, grammar, or vocabulary is known as a <u>dialect</u>. A collection of similar dialects (usually mutually intelligible) form a <u>language</u>. In this view, therefore, a dialect is any distinctively differentiated variety of a language. All languages have dialects, and it is important to note that everyone speaks a dialect (there is no such thing as a "pure" form of a language as opposed to dialects).

Dialects come about, then, because different norms in pronunciation, grammar, and vocabulary arise in the usage of groups who are separated by geography or social boundaries.[1] The Navajo-speaking child will learn to call 'snow' <u>zas</u> in Toadlena, New Mexico, and <u>yas</u> in Greasewood, Arizona. The Spanish-speaking child will learn to pronounce <u>calle</u> as /kalye/ in Peru, /kaye/ in Mexico, and /kae/ in parts of Texas and the Southwest. And the English-speaking child will learn to carry water in a <u>pail</u> in Boston, Massachusetts, but in a <u>bucket</u> in Austin, Texas. Such differences are normal and inevitable, and have their roots in the very nature of child language learning. Although the recent influence of mass communication and rapid transportation has done much to retard the forces of dialect differentiation, these forces remain most powerful precisely during the early years, when an individual's basic linguistic habits are being fixed, and hence will never be entirely offset.

For a variety of social, economic, and political reasons, some groups of speakers in a country will enjoy higher social prestige than others, and because of this, their dialect(s) will often come to be considered "better" than others. The judgment of relative "value" of different dialects is a purely social one, however, and has nothing to do with the inherent qualities of the dialects themselves. No dialect is inherently better or more adequate or more logical than another, just as no language is inherently superior to any other.

In most literate societies, the dialect spoken by the upper classes of educated speakers in the most important urban center(s) becomes the de facto "standard" dialect, and is used as the basis for the written form of the language. Other dialects, lacking wider prestige and the support of the printed word, come to be considered as "nonstandard." It should be emphasized that they are just as complete and systematic as the "standard" dialect, and that it is only a matter of historical accident that one, rather than another, dialect becomes the "standard."

---

[1] These changes are cumulative, so that if groups originally speaking the same language remain isolated from one another long enough, their dialects will become mutually unintelligible languages. In this way Latin as spoken in the several former Roman provinces has become modern Spanish, French, Italian, Portuguese, and Rumanian. Similarly, English, Dutch, German, Swedish, Danish, and Norwegian are the latter-day dialects of an original Germanic language. And of course each of these languages has its own regional and social dialects today. Latin and Germanic were themselves ultimately dialects of yet an earlier language, usually called Indo-European, which was also ancestral to Slavic, Celtic, Greek, Sanskrit, Persian, and Hittite. A group of languages so related is often referred to as a "language family."

Far from being corruptions of the standard dialect, they are in fact sister dialects, each with its own history. Many of the features of nonstandard dialects represent usages which were once common to all, but which have passed out of fashion among upper class urban speakers, while surviving in the countryside and among the less economically advantaged. Examples from English would be the double negative (which goes back to King Alfred and is still standard in Spanish: cf. I don't have nothing and No tengo nada), and the pronunciation of deaf to rhyme with leaf (which was used by Noah Webster). Examples from Spanish would include asina for así 'thus', which is found in Old Spanish, onde for donde 'where', which is common in sixteenth century documents, and vide for ví 'I saw', which was used by Julius Caesar (Vini, vide, vici—I came, I saw, I conquered').[2] The speaker of a nonstandard dialect is not "confused" or "wrong" when his speech differs from the standard dialect, but he is actually using a different system.

Since each dialect is a system, any attempt to teach a standard dialect to a speaker of a nonstandard dialect should employ a systematic approach if it is to succeed in helping the student acquire productive control over the new forms. At the same time, an approach which stigmatizes the student's own speech should be avoided, since this will simply serve to humiliate him and create an environment which is not conducive to learning. The recognition of the nature of dialect differences is important in any educational program, but it is doubly so in a bilingual program, since in addition to teaching students a second language, they must in many cases at the same time be taught a second dialect of their own language. In addition, the student's own dialect may affect the nature of the problems he will have in learning the second language, so that teaching materials may have to be adjusted accordingly.

As a person develops his control over his own native language, the linguistic habits involved in the perception and production of the language gradually become increasingly fixed. Although all physiologi-

---

[2] It is commonplace to encounter descriptions of the Spanish spoken in Texas as "not a language," or as "a random mixture of English and Spanish, having no grammar," and to hear it stigmatized with the label "Tex-Mex." Several recent studies (Lance 1969; González 1970) have documented the falsity of these claims, by showing that Texas Spanish is simply a variety of the North Mexican Spanish dialect, with a fully developed grammatical and phonological system, and distinguished only by the relatively larger number of English loanwords it has adopted (e.g., troca 'truck', which, however, is also found in Northern Mexico).

cally normal children are born with the capacity to produce any sound used in any language, as their practice with the sounds of their own language proceeds, they lose the flexibility to produce other sounds. More importantly in some respects, they learn to hear all sounds in terms of the particular set of phonetic categories (the phonemes) used in their own language (or more precisely, in a particular dialect of that language). "Foreign" sounds are not heard as such, but rather are unconsciously and automatically pigeonholed in one of the pre-existing categories of the native language. Spanish speakers, for example, commonly hear English ship and sheep as identical, because the differences in these vowel sounds are not made in Spanish. Navajo speakers have difficulty in discriminating such English words as pear and bear, and for the same reason, namely, that Navajo does not differentiate between the consonants p and b. English speakers, conversely, commonly have difficulty in recognizing the difference between the r-sounds in Spanish pero 'but' and perro 'dog', and usually hear the Navajo consonant sound in the middle of hooghan 'home' as an English g. It is not that they are inherently incapable of hearing the particular differences, but rather that they have been conditioned not to, by their previous experience with their own language.

Comparable problems occur in grammar and vocabulary, all of which result from the natural tendency of a speaker to carry over the habits of his native language into the second, or to translate directly from the one into the other. Where distinctions exist in the second language which are not found in the native language, such as (for English speakers learning Spanish) the difference between the imperfect and preterite tenses in Spanish (vs. the English past tense), or the distinction between ser and estar (vs. English be), these will often not be recognized and will lead to mistakes in grammar or meaning. All of these problems of perception and use of a second language which arise from the native language habits of the speaker are termed interference. In order to be able to recognize and deal effectively with problems of interference when they occur in the classroom, the teacher in a bilingual program needs to know the differences between the two languages involved, and what teaching strategies to adopt in particular situations. In addition, if bilingual instruction is to be efficient and effective, the preparation of materials and the organization of the curriculum itself must rely heavily on information about potential points of interference between the two languages.

We often tend to think of learning a new language as simply learning new words to express our concepts. Learning a language is actually far more complex, for a language is composed of more than just words and their meanings. Language is an integrated system of phonology, grammar, and lexicon. We acquired control over the phonology and grammar of our native language quite unconsciously, and almost entirely within our own preschool years. It is understandable, then, for most people to remember only the conscious and most recent aspect of their own language development—vocabulary building—and to be largely unaware of the other aspects of language learning.

We must recognize that each language is a total system for transmitting meaning, and beware of the subtle fallacy that direct translation between languages is possible. Such a view is fostered by our traditional textbooks, with their seemingly clear-cut English/Spanish (Navajo, etc.) word glossaries, but this view is simplistic and misleading. Each language categorizes the world of experience differently, and requires its speakers to specify certain aspects of their observation and to leave others unspecified or optionally specifiable.

The color spectrum, for instance, is arbitrarily divided by speakers of English into eight basic colors, whereas Navajo speakers combine the area covered roughly by English blue and green into one category labeled dotł?ish. Verbs of motion are also categorized quite differently in English and Navajo, and no direct translation is possible from one system to the other: English verbs are categorized according to such factors as direction, type, rate, and source of movement; Navajo verbs of motion are categorized according to the shape of the object moved. The English verb give would be translated by a different Navajo verb with each of the following referents: sheet of paper, book, baby, babies, cigarette, rope, wool, and mud. To translate I am putting the ball on the table and I am putting the pencil on the table, Navajo will use entirely different verb forms reflecting the different shapes of the objects. Conversely, Navajo will use the same verb form in expressing I am putting the ball on the table and The sun is moving across the sky, because sun and ball are both grammatically categorized as "round objects."

Further, since the meaning of words is also deeply influenced by culture, it is important to realize that a word-for-word "literal" translation can never be complete, and may often be misleading. An example of this is the translation of English hot dog as Spanish perro caliente. Of a more serious nature, faulty translation between Navajo and English has lead to erroneously diagnosed physical ailments, the relinquishment of children for adoption by parents who thought they would be given foster care, and, at an earlier time in history, even bloody battles.

Not all translation problems have such dramatic consequences, but occasionally misunderstanding and even embarrassment result from the different meanings words have in different languages or dialects. A speaker often does not realize which words in a new language are offensive until he tries them out and gets a negative reaction from native speakers. A student learning English may not be aware of the attitude toward the term for 'female dog', nor the student learning Spanish that huevo has taken on the meaning 'testicle' in Mexico, and that blanquillo is the more acceptable term for 'egg'. Differences in social acceptability and effect can be seen between the Spanish expression Dios mío and its English translation 'My God', which is much stronger. Another example is the Spanish use of Jesús as a common given name and the English view of this practice as disrespectful (Lado, 1957).

Misunderstanding occurs frequently as a result of students' failure to recognize (and of teachers' failure to point out) that words do not have fixed unitary meanings, but that the meaning is often relative to the context. Examples are the different meanings of such common lexical items as run and can in different contexts. In addition, problems encountered by speakers of closely related languages are the "false friends"—words which sound alike but have different meanings. A common example of such confusion is the asistir of Spanish, which means 'to attend'. Because of the similar form, speakers of Spanish sometimes use assist when they mean attend in English.

Different social conventions which are reflected in language must also be considered, such as the Navajo child's speaking softly and avoiding eye contact to show respect. The teacher who demands that the student look at him and talk louder is making a mistake. Group attitudes must also be considered. Teachers of many American Indian groups have found that traditional methods of motivating children to compete for grades does not work, when competition is not considered a desirable trait within the culture. An example of the type of unfortunate cross-cultural misunderstanding which can occur was observed when a Navajo second-grader called her teacher grandmother, which is a title of respect in the Navajo language. The teacher, not understanding this, laughed at the child and tried to correct her. Such lack of understanding of the cultures which are reflected in the native languages of the children can reduce the effectiveness of any educational program.

Psychological factors

Every normal child is born with a built-in capacity—indeed, what amounts to a biological imperative—to acquire language. Each child, with very little direct instruction, works out and internalizes the system, or grammar, of the language which he hears around him. This is true in all societies, from the simplest to the technologically most advanced, whether literate or not. How the child does this is far from understood, but he accomplishes this seeming miracle largely between the ages of two and six. By the time he comes to school, then, he will have developed control over some 80 per cent of the grammar (and sound system) of his native language. What dialect he acquires will be largely determined by the region (and social class) in which he grows up.

At the same time, of course, his intellectual ability is developing; and he is learning how to behave in his society—even learning how to learn, which is not the same in all societies (Center for Applied Linguistics, 1968). Culture-free nonverbal intelligence tests, such as the Goodenough-Harris Draw-a-Man Test, show that various maturational faculties develop at roughly the same rate in all populations, and are therefore universal. Concept formation likewise proceeds apace, affected at least in part by the specific category-distinctions (of shape, color, size, etc.) recognized in the native language.

The statement is often encountered that economic deprivation and associated social conditions tend to retard the development of language and intelligence in the child. While this may be true, such claims need to be treated skeptically, since poor performance on various tests—particularly where the child is from a culturally and linguistically different group—may simply reflect the cultural and linguistic bias of the test. For example, even very intelligent first-graders in rural Southern California are unable to identify the pictures of <u>furnace</u> and <u>fire escape</u> used in one well-known intelligence test, because they have never seen such objects, while Indian children on a reservation in New Mexico experience similar difficulties with pictures depicting "familiar" aspects of urban experience. Yet other strengths and abilities which these children may have acquired from their own experience frequently go uncredited, simply because the tests are not designed to measure them. The range of cultural backgrounds represented in bilingual programs further lowers the reliability rating which may be placed on verbal intelligence scores as measured by presently available instruments.

Verbal IQ tests are notorious for the distorted results they give when used with children lacking a full native command of English. What the tests actually measure under such circumstances is knowledge of English rather than intelligence, as shown by the frequent dramatic rise in many non-English speaking children's IQ scores after only a year of schooling. Yet every year, thousands of nonnative English speakers are placed in classes for the retarded because of a failure to recognize the reason for their low scores on such tests. Not only is this an affront to the self-esteem of the child, but teachers in these classes are not prepared to recognize the special needs of such children, and lack the training to give them appropriate work in English.

Even IQ tests which are in the language of the student may not be free of the cultural bias as mentioned above, since they are often merely direct translations from an English test. In addition, they are rarely standardized, and may fail to take dialect differences into account—just as their English counterparts fail to do. It was found in California, for example, that not even college students who spoke

Spanish as their native language knew some of the items on a Spanish IQ test which had been developed in Texas for use with first-graders.

Studies of the effect of bilingualism on intelligence are distorted by all of the factors just discussed, but they are further called into question because of their failure to match the subject populations socioeconomically. In general, bilingual subjects have been from a lower socioeconomic group, while monolingual subjects have been from a higher (middle or upper middle class) group. This imbalance has naturally tended to prejudice the results of these studies. In one of the few studies which carefully matched individual bilingual and monolingual subjects as closely as possible, it was shown that the bilingual subjects performed as well as the monolinguals in all areas, and exceeded their performance in certain types of tasks involving symbolic manipulation and flexibility of response (Peal and Lambert, 1962).

Up to this point we have been speaking as though bilingualism were a unitary phenomenon. However, most students of the subject recognize two major types, which have been called <u>coordinate</u> and <u>compound</u> bilingualism. The difference may be illustrated by the following diagrams:

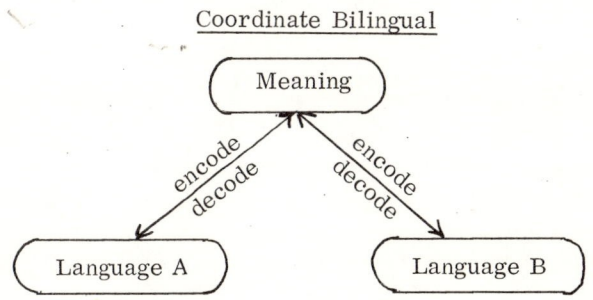

Coordinate Bilingual

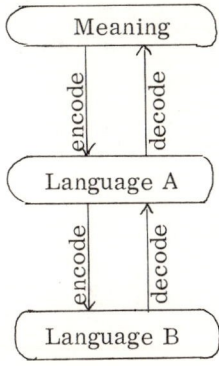

Compound Bilingual

In the coordinate bilingual the two languages operate as independent systems for the encoding and decoding of information. The coordinate bilingual can understand or say things in either language, but he may not be able to translate between the languages on a word-for-word basis. The compound bilingual, on the other hand, formulates his thoughts first in one language (usually his native one) and then goes through a high-speed translation process into the second language. Similarly, messages received in the second language are translated back into the first language before their meaning can be apprehended. The translation process may operate so rapidly and at such a low conscious level that the speaker is not even aware of it, but it is not uncommon to find in the compound bilingual's production of the second language many examples of grammatical and lexical interference from his first language.

The two types of bilingualism just sketched are extremes, and there are many degrees of variation in between, so that few bilinguals would be purely one or the other type. But the distinction is a useful one, and correlates well with two kinds of language-learning situations. A coordinate bilingual has typically learned his two (or more) languages in separate functional contexts, where it was necessary to learn each language for communication in specific situations, and little or no direct translation was possible (e.g., home vs. playmates, parents vs. grandparents, etc.). Each language then is learned as an independent communication system. The compound bilingual, on the other hand, has typically learned his second language in school, where it was presented on a translation-equivalence basis. In addition, it is often the case that the compound bilingual has learned his second language following the onset of puberty, and in a setting which encouraged a translation approach.

There are many factors outside the direct control of the school which influence first and second-language development. These include:

1. The nature of the child's preschool linguistic environment.
2. Personality traits of parents and their attitudes.
3. Degree of association with adults.
4. Child-rearing practices in the home.
5. Number of siblings, and ordinal rank among them.
6. The attitude of the parents toward their own speech community and toward the second-language group.

The importance of home and family to growth in language fluency is readily recognized by educators, and many have worked for better understanding, respect, and cooperation between home and school. Bilingual education can hopefully succeed in bridging the linguistic gap which has often prevented such a relationship, and in addition may help to break down linguistic and social barriers between language groups in communities. By reducing prejudice and increasing mutual understanding, therefore, a bilingual program can contribute to the development of a healtheir and more cooperative community spirit.

The remarkable capacity for language learning which children bring to bear in learning their first language continues largely unabated until the onset of puberty, after which it declines sharply in most people, apparently as a result of complex physical and chemical changes in the brain. A bilingual program, by beginning early, seeks to exploit this natural capacity in the child. But whereas the child has spent all of his waking hours for four years in the task of mastering his native language, the school may not have more than a few hours each day to bring the child to the same level of competence in the second language. It is for this reason, therefore, that the presentation of sounds, structure, and vocabulary must be made in a way which as efficiently as possible short-cuts the time required for learning the second language.

Equally important is motivation. From a child's point of view, the desire to communicate is one of the strongest motivations for learning a language. For this reason, there should be as much opportunity for inter-pupil communication as possible. Bilingual programs which assign English-speaking children to one classroom and non-English-speaking children to another are failing to utilize one of the most powerful psychological factors in language learning.

Learning may also be affected by ideas concerning the appropriateness of becoming bilingual. In the United States, it is now usually assumed that a child will become bilingual if English is not his native language, but English-speaking children are often handicapped by lower expectations in this regard from school and community. This view is likely to change with the widespread acceptance of bilingual education.

Since learning to use a language involves a type of skill formation, practice is essential to success. Fortunately, children enjoy the kind of organized discipline which is involved in many language-teaching activities—repetition, choral response, even rote memorization—so that some of the motivation to learn can come from doing what is enjoyable. The administrator should be forewarned, therefore, that in a good language program the students, not the teacher, will be talking much of the time, and that a successful bilingual classroom will not be a quiet classroom.

Social and cultural factors

Language is a social phenomenon; language would not even exist if men were not social animals who must communicate in order to cooperate. And language is always learned in a social context, from other members of the society. All language teachers need therefore to have some understanding of both cultures reflected in the languages of instruction, and of their interrelationships. School districts contemplating or already implementing bilingual programs should attempt to gain information on the sociolinguistic situation in their area. This can be done by formulating a questionnaire to determine facts about the following points:

1. Who uses each language?
2. Where?
3. When?
4. With whom?
5. Why? For what purpose?
6. How? In what manner or style?
7. About what?
8. With what result?
9. What attitudes are expressed concerning the use of the languages and about the speakers of each?
10. How do the different segments of the community feel about their children acquiring both languages?

A knowledge of the type of language used in the community for various purposes can help educators set realistic language objectives for the children. In bilingual communities, each language is often considered appropriate for certain topics and not for others. This situation is sometimes called <u>diglossia</u>, and creates a need for students to develop a somewhat different range of skills in each language. Balanced bilinguals are usually found in situations where both languages are used for all kinds of experiences.

As the second language of the community is brought into the schools in bilingual education, the range of concepts and experiences which may immediately be built upon in the native language depends in part on the contexts in which that language has been used at home and in the community. What language has been used when shopping for groceries, when visiting the doctor or health clinic, when attending Sunday school or church? What language is heard on radio and television?

Most bilinguals live among other bilinguals and may have contact with only one, or possibly no, monolingual speech community. Children of Spanish- and English-speaking parents may know only English words, and yet pronounce them in the Spanish phonological system and using Spanish syntax. Children of Navajo and English-speaking parents may have been taught only English words at home, but with the glottal stops and simplified consonant clusters of their bilingual parents. When two languages are used in a community, the lexicon may be partly shared and the resulting linguistic system may differ from each language as it is spoken in monolingual communities.

Children usually learn whatever language or languages they hear in their home and neighborhood because of their need for communication and group membership. They need language to ask questions and to play. A bilingual program has a much better chance for success if the children need both languages to communicate in or out of school and have a continuous exposure to them.

There are possible social consequences to being bilingual which need to be recognized. Major conflicts in values may arise. In a traditional English-dominant school system, one of the first impressions a non-English-speaking child may have is that people in authority do not speak his language. From the beginning, he may perceive a conflict between family and friends vs. the school system. In addition, the language the child uses will influence how he perceives himself and how he is perceived in the community, since language use is often an important badge of group membership identification. Switching languages may be accepted as natural, or it may arouse the suspicion of others and be seen as a type of secrecy, or as a rejection of the native culture. Conversely, the teacher may interpret the child's use of his native language as a rejection of the majority culture, and may react with hostility toward the child.

This perception by others is very important, for the attitudes of the home and community toward bilingualism and toward the respective language groups affects to a great extent the attitudes of the students. These attitudes in turn are important for motivation and achievement in second-language learning. These attitudinal factors affect the child's perception of himself and his language in relation to school and the majority (or minority) group and its language. It is not uncommon to find children from Spanish-speaking homes denying that they know any Spanish, since the long repression of the language in school and the generally subordinate social status of Spanish speakers have made them ashamed of their linguistic and cultural heritage. But the use of the home language as a medium of instruction in school gives it a status of prestige, and enhances the child's self-respect and self-confidence at the same time. Importantly, its use helps the child in adjusting to the essentially alien situation of the classroom. Children who would be fearful and withdrawn find help, support, and guidance, and are better able to make the transition to become participative and active learners. Significantly also, the attitude of English-speaking students to their nonnative English-speaking classmates often changes from one of condescension or rejection to one of admiration and acceptance when the latter have an opportunity to act as "experts" and help "teach" their language to their English-speaking peers.

A good bilingual program is almost of necessity a bicultural program as well. Both affectively and cognitively, culture is inseparable from the language which is used to articulate it. The recognition in the school of the child's native cultural heritage can do a great deal to enhance his self-esteem. As it may help him to adjust to the culture shock of the unfamiliar school environment, it may also help him to develop a more positive attitude toward the school. The development of such an attitude can be a determining factor in his eventual scholastic success.

In the past the majority culture has developed negative stereotypes of the members of minority cultures, and these stereotypes—many of them held by teachers—have been imposed on the minority cultures. These stereotypes are familiar in such terms as lazy, dirty, unreliable, untrustworthy, and ignorant, often applied to such groups. In many cases, the stereotype is transmitted to the student in the school, both from the teacher and from his majority-group classmates, with the result that he develops a strongly negative self-image which is inimical to successful achievement in school. A cultural component of a bilingual program which teaches respect for and acceptance of the cultural values of the minority group, and which informs the child about his own cultural heritage, goes a long way toward building pride and self-confidence in the child, and lays the foundation for his growth as a secure, well-balanced adult who can make a positive contribution to our society.

SELECTED BIBLIOGRAPHY

Diebold, A. Richard, Jr. 1966. The consequences of early bilingualism in cognitive development and personality formation. ERIC No. ED 020 491.
Ervin-Tripp, Susan. 1968. Becoming a bilingual. ERIC No. ED 018 786.
Fishman, Joshua A. 1969. Bilingual attitudes and behaviors. Language sciences. Bloomington, Indiana University Research Center for the Language Sciences.
_____, ed. 1968. Readings in the sociology of language. The Hague, Mouton.
González, Gustavo. 1970. The acquisition of Spanish grammar by native Spanish speakers. Austin, Texas, The University of Texas at Austin. Doctoral dissertation.
Jones, W. 1960. A critical study of bilingualism and nonverbal intelligence. British journal of educational psychology XXX, I: 71-77.
Lado, Robert. 1957. Linguistics across cultures. Ann Arbor, Michigan, The University of Michigan Press.
Lance, Donald M. 1969. A brief study of Spanish-English bilingualism: final report. College Station, Texas, Texas A & M University. ERIC No. ED 032 529.

Lieberman, Philip. 1967. Intonation, perception, and language. Cambridge, MIT Press.
McNeill, David. 1967. The development of language. ERIC No. ED 017 921.
Peal, E. and Wallace Lambert. 1962. The relation of bilingualism to intelligence. Psychological monographs: general and applied LXXVI, 27: 1-23.
Saporta, Sol. 1961. Psycholinguistics: a book of readings. New York, Holt, Rinehart, and Winston.
Styles of learning among American Indians: an outline for research. 1968. Washington, D.C., Center for Applied Linguistics.

NOTE: ERIC (Educational Resources Information Center) publications orders should be placed by ED number and not by title or author. These are available in either hard copy or microfiche. Order from:

ERIC Document Reproduction Service
P.O. Box 190
Arlington, Virginia 22210

CHAPTER III

DESIGN

The primary responsibility for the initiation of bilingual education programs in a school district lies with the school board and the superintendent. If they feel such a program warrants serious consideration, a suggested first step would be to appoint a representative advisory committee to study school and community conditions and decide on the feasibility of such an innovation. The function of the committee would be to provide liaison with the various elements in the community, and to conduct a survey (as suggested in "social factors" above) to gather information on:

> the linguistic composition of the community;
> the socioeconomic status of speakers of each language;
> their educational achievement levels;
> their attitudes toward bilingual education.

At this stage an estimate can also be made of:

> the cost of implementing a bilingual program;
> the availability of facilities, materials, and trained personnel in the district;
> financial resources.

If the advisory committee, school board, and superintendent now feel that they are ready for a bilingual program, the next step would be to appoint a program coordinator. This is a vital person to the project, and the following qualifications should be considered:

> Is he a fluent speaker of both languages?
> Is he sensitive to public relations?
> Does he understand children, schools, linguistics, anthropology, psychology, curriculum design, evaluation, and the principles of research?

The position of coordinator is fully as demanding as the qualifications suggest, since he will be responsible for:

recommending principles, objectives, and program organization to the school board;
recruiting bilingual teachers, aides, consultants and other personnel;
conducting pre-service and in-service training of teachers and aides;
curriculum design;
materials preparation, selection, and adaptation;
plan of evaluation;
contacts with state and federal agencies concerned;
public relations.

The purpose of the bilingual education program must be decided on before a specific plan is selected. Every effort should be made to secure the consultant services of a trained linguist at this critical point in the planning. The following sources of information may be utilized during the planning stages regarding professional resources:

English as a Second Language Program
Center for Applied Linguistics
1611 North Kent Street
Arlington, Virginia 22209

Teachers of English to Speakers of Other Languages (TESOL)
James E. Alatis, Executive Secretary
School of Languages and Linguistics
Georgetown University
Washington, D.C. 20057

Executive Secretary
National Council of Teachers of English
1111 Kenyon Road
Urbana, Illinois 61801

Educational Resources Information Center (ERIC)
Center for Applied Linguistics
1611 North Kent Street
Arlington, Virginia 22209

Administrators have several alternatives in program design to choose from when setting up a program. In making a choice, they should take several factors into account, including the community situation, school resources, and their basic purposes for initiating a bilingual education program. One desirable plan would devote most of the school day to instruction in the native language during the kindergarten, first and second grades, and equal portions to both languages from third through eighth grades.

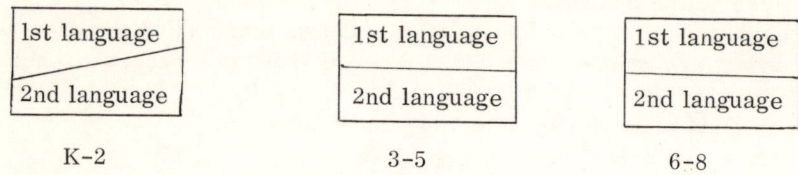

In the early years, work in the second language would be focused primarily on developing linguistic skills (in grammar, pronunciation, and vocabulary), and would use special second-language teaching methods. The program would gradually phase into use of the second language as a medium of instruction and would pursue the development of language arts skills in both languages.

Such a plan would be recommended where the school is in or near a bilingual community and students would have the opportunity to use both languages in and out of school. Even if they speak only one language when they enter school in such an area, the second language will probably not sound entirely strange to them.

A balanced bilingual program such as the one diagrammed above requires bilingual teachers and aides, and instructional materials in both languages. It is not necessary, and probably not even desirable, for the same subjects to be taught in two languages. Reading should be introduced in the children's first language, and it is therefore obvious that such reading readiness skills as the recognition of sound-symbol relationships should also be introduced in the first language. Transfer to reading the second language <u>should not</u> be made until initial reading skills are well established—usually during the second grade. <u>If local regulations specify reading achievement tests only in English before that time, they should be adjusted to allow for bilingual education.</u> Whatever the dominant language of the child, mathematical computational skills should be first developed in English since advanced work in mathematics will probably be done in this language and later switching of these skills is difficult. The other language can and should be used for non-computational purposes (recognition of number words, simple counting, giving addresses, etc.).

Most concept development in such areas as science and social studies will probably take place in the dominant language of the children. Concepts need not be developed a second time in the second language, but new labels may be provided for them. A child who learns science in Spanish, for instance, may have English terms for the same concepts introduced during the ESL (English as a Second Language) period as partial content for the English language lessons. When concepts are taught twice, children tend to "tune out" the lessons in their second language; they learn not to listen, because they don't need to. Just having more labels provided in the second language does not seem to have this negative effect, and allows the children more flexibility in the event they later transfer to a school without a bilingual program or one in which the schedule provides for different language divisions.

Some subjects, such as music, art, and physical education, can be taught to all children in both languages, but even here it is best to minimize interference between the linguistic systems and use only one language during any one class period.

An example of a daily schedule for first grade follows. This class is composed both of students whose dominant language is Spanish (Group A) and whose dominant language is English (Group B). The teacher is assumed to be bilingual. Particularly if no aide is available, a team teaching arrangement might be desirable.

	Group A	Group B
8:00-8:20	Opening activities (Spanish one week, English the next)	
8:20-8:45	Reading group with teacher in Spanish	Seat work supervised by aide, work on letter names, or other activities developing reading skills in English
8:45-9:00	Seat work supervised by aide, work on letter names, or other activities developing reading skills, in Spanish	Reading group with teacher in English
9:00-9:10	Break	
9:10-9:30	English as a Second Language (ESL)	Spanish as a Second Language (SSL)
9:30-10:00	Arithmetic in English	
10:00-10:30	Physical Education	
10:30-11:00	Science with teacher in Spanish	Handwriting with aide

	Group A	Group B
11:00-11:30	Handwriting with aide	Science with teacher in English
11:30-12:30	Lunch	
12:30-1:00	Social Studies with teacher in Spanish	SSL (reinforcement of concepts in second language with aide) while practicing new language patterns
1:00-1:30	ESL (Reinforcement of concepts in second language with aide) while practicing new language patterns	Social Studies with teacher in English
1:30-2:30	Art, Music, Literature	

Scheduling might be easier in some respects if all Spanish-speaking children were assigned to one classroom and all English-speaking children to another, but such administrative divisions often remain in effect on the playground and in the community and deprive the children of the motivation to learn and practice the second language in order to communicate with friends.

If the purpose of the program is only to make non-English-speaking children bilingual, more time can be devoted to instruction in English and the native language maintained in some subject area. The curriculum could be visualized as follows:

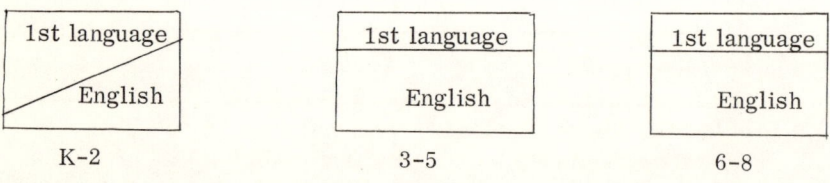

In this plan, the first language of the children would still be used for initial reading instruction with the transfer to reading in English delayed until second grade. This design is feasible for districts which lack sufficient bilingual personnel or resources to make a more balanced program possible, or in communities where the advantages of bilingual education have not been recognized.

When the social situation indicates that it is more expedient to move toward rapid acculturation, with bilingual instruction utilized only to convert the students from one linguistic medium to another, the following plan might be followed:

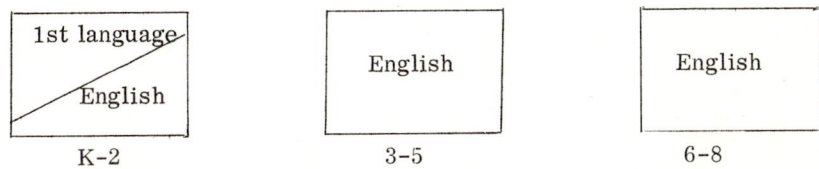

This type of program is less desirable than the others, but might be dictated by local conditions and available resources. It should be remembered, however, that to qualify as a bilingual program, at least one content area must be taught in each language. Proposals to merely teach English as a second language and not utilize the students' native language as a medium of instruction are not currently being considered for funding under Title VII, the Bilingual Education Act.

One of the biggest problems facing pioneering bilingual programs is the shortage of suitably trained teachers. Most bilingual teachers have received their own education and training entirely in English, and may experience some difficulty learning to teach in their native language. They have to teach subjects in a language other than the one in which they originally learned about them, and there is a shortage of helpful books and guidelines. It should be strongly emphasized that a teacher is not adequately qualified to teach a language merely because it is his native tongue. The following requirements should be considered by those hiring teachers for bilingual education programs:

willingness to participate in an innovative program;
knowledge of the structures of both languages of instruction;
general understanding of the nature of language, including the acceptability and inevitability of dialect variations in all living languages;
specific understanding of his own dialect and the dialect of the area in which he teaches;
knowledge of methods for teaching a second language;
understanding and acceptance of all cultures represented in the community;
knowledge of the growth and development patterns of children;
competence to provide a good linguistic model, preferably in both languages. If a teacher is competent in only one language, he should be placed in a team-teaching situation, and should not teach in his weak language.

Teachers and aides for a new program may profitably be hired for the summer preceding the first year of bilingual instruction. During these months the program coordinator, with assistance from specialized consultants from universities, educational service centers, or state educational agencies, can conduct a training and preparation program, which would include the following areas:

linguistics;
second language methodology;
curriculum design;
review and adaptation of available instructional material;
creation of new material;
practice teaching in a language other than English;
study of the cultures represented in the community, including their languages, beliefs, child-rearing practices, family structures, motivating forces, and coping styles.

Principals of schools involved in the program, and teachers in the next grade level, should also be included in all planning and orientation sessions. It is crucial to the success of a program to have their sympathetic support and cooperation. Administrators, who may have to explain the program to outsiders, or who may have to make decisions regarding the use of specially-devised local achievement tests in place of state-approved tests, need to have information about the program, its goals, and its methods. Teachers from immediately succeeding grade levels need the same information, for they need to begin preparing well in advance to adjust their teaching and their expectations to fit the students they will receive the following year. A failure to adequately inform either group, by arousing unnecessary anxieties, may jeopardize the success of any program.

Community cooperation is vital to the success of bilingual education programs, primarily because of the effect its attitude will have on the language learning of the children. It is therefore very important for the schools to communicate with the community at all stages of planning and implementation. The purpose is not to sell a program, but to inform and promote understanding. If the majority in the community is unwilling to accept bilingual education, it may be possible to find a group which will accept it, at least for experimental purposes. Direct observation of the results of bilingual education will convince most people that it is sound policy, and the program can then be expanded. A variety of media can be used to keep the community informed:

open meeting of school board in early stages with expert in bilingual education present to answer questions;

DESIGN / 31

 news and feature items for newspapers, radio, and television in
   both languages;
 speakers available for PTA's, service clubs, or church groups
   (the presentation should always be made in the dominant language of the group);
 small pamphlet describing purposes and plans (prepared in both
   languages) and distributed in grocery stores, churches, health
   clinics, and wherever it is likely to reach all segments of the
   community;
 special invitations to leaders of all segments to observe planning
   and training sessions and early phases of classroom instruction;
 open invitation to all members of the community (once the program
   is under way) to come to see what is going on in _their_ schools;
 a newsletter sent home with students at regular intervals, including pictures of activities;
 continuing communication between the school and community regarding both progress and problems.

   One of the most beneficial results of bilingual programs may well be the extent to which it allows parents to become involved in the formal education of their children. An example of such community involvement and support may be seen at the Rough Rock Demonstration School on the Navajo reservation, which has already had a functional bilingual program for several years. Parents and preschool siblings visit classes freely, join the students for lunch (which often consists of mutton stew and fry bread), or sit quietly in the halls—a visible and comforting part of the school environment. In one room, a Navajo mother shows the young children how to make fry bread; in another, a grandfather tells a story in Navajo to a group of young listeners; in a third, a grandmother sits near her loom in a corner, carding wool as she listens to the arithmetic lesson in progress. It is not surprising that the Navajo name for Rough Rock means "The People's School."
   Administrators and teachers must work to bridge the traditional cultural gap between English-speaking schools and non-English-speaking homes. It is the job of the school to let the parents know that their participation is wanted, that it is indeed needed, and to provide opportunities for communication. Some of the following steps may encourage parental involvement:

 notices and invitations in the language of the home;
 different and more convenient meeting times for PTA or similar
   activities;
 representation from all community groups in school-related organ-
   izations or councils;

requests for help in preparing instructional materials (periodic group work sessions have been very successful when coffee is served, baby sitting provided, and a brief presentation is made of the progress of the program and the way the materials the parents are helping prepare—games, flash cards, flannel board stories, etc. —will be used in the classrooms);
encouragement for parents to visit school at any time.

One of the most important factors in promoting parental involvement and better understanding between home and school is inherent in the nature of a bilingual program. The children are taught in the language of the home, and can express or apply what they have learned there. Furthermore, the parents are in a better position to understand what is going on at school, and to provide important support for the education of their children.

Any educational program should be based on the principle that the school takes the cultural and language experiences the child brings with him and builds upon these. Beginning instruction through the medium of the child's native language is not only sound from the standpoint of increased educational efficiency; in such a program, the child and his culture are recognized as worthy of consideration. Giving him pride in his cultural heritage will at once help him to improve his self-image and increase his success potential, so that he will better be able to benefit from what the educational system has to offer him.

SELECTED BIBLIOGRAPHY

Andersson, Theodore and Mildred Boyer. 1970. Bilingual schooling in the United States. Austin, Texas, Southwest Educational Development Laboratory. (For sale by the Superintendent of Documents, U.S. Government Printing Office, Washington, D.C. 20402. Six dollars per set of two volumes.)

Mackey, William F. 1969. A typology of bilingual education. Report prepared for a research conference on bilingual education under the auspices of the USOE Bureau of Research.

Past, Ray et al. 1966. Bilingualism—from the viewpoint of recruitment and preparation of bilingual teachers. Paper presented at the annual conference of the Southwest Council of Foreign Language Teachers, El Paso, Texas, Nov. 4-5, 1966. ERIC No. ED 018 297.

Perren, G. E., ed. 1968. Teachers of English as a second language: their training and preparation. New York, Cambridge University Press. ERIC No. ED 023 087.

University resources in the United States and Canada for the study of linguistics, 1969-1970. 1970. Washington, D.C., Center for Applied Linguistics.

CHAPTER IV

THE LANGUAGES OF INSTRUCTION

Phonology

Every language (and dialect of a language) uses a limited number of classes of sounds to signal the differences between words. The number of such distinctive sounds, called phonemes, ranges from as few as sixteen (in Hawaiian) to around sixty (in Circassian, a Caucasian language), with English standing about half-way between these extremes. In order to understand the pronunciation problems of children in a bilingual program, the teacher needs to have a good understanding of the way speech sounds are made, and the differences in the sound systems of English and the other language used in the program. In addition, some knowledge of dialectal and developmental differences in the phonological systems of the two languages involved is important.

A student of any age learning English must learn to hear, and then produce, twenty-four distinctive consonant sounds.[1] These phonemes are classified according to the way they are pronounced, as <u>stops</u>, <u>affricates</u>, <u>fricatives</u> (sometimes called spirants), <u>resonants</u>, and <u>nasals</u>. In the following chart, each phoneme is illustrated by an example in conventional orthography.

	Voiceless	Voiced
<u>Stops</u> (sounds produced by complete closing of the passage of air through the mouth):	/p/ <u>p</u>ie /t/ <u>t</u>ie /k/ <u>c</u>at	/b/ <u>b</u>oy /d/ <u>d</u>og /g/ <u>g</u>ate

---

[1] The symbol used for each of these phonemes is enclosed in slanted lines (/ /), and is often not the same as the symbol which represents the sound in conventional spelling. Some sounds in English are spelled in several ways, as the /f/ sound in <u>f</u>ear, <u>ph</u>oto, and enou<u>gh</u>. The system of notation used here allows one symbol to consistently represent one distinctive sound.

		Voiceless	Voiced
Affricates (stop consonants released with a friction sound):		/č/ chair	/ǰ/ giant
Fricatives (produced by a constriction causing friction in the mouth but not completely closing the passage of air):		/f/ fair /θ/ thing /s/ sit /š/ shell /h/ house	/v/ very /ð/ this /z/ zebra /ž/ azure
Resonants (produced without friction; /w/ and /y/ are often called semivowels or glides):			/w/ wash /y/ yellow /l/ light /r/ rat
Nasals (produced with the stream of air flowing through the nasal passage rather than through the mouth):			/m/ man /n/ name /ŋ/ sing

Vowel sounds are classified according to where they are produced in the mouth, as <u>high</u>, <u>mid</u>, or <u>low</u>, and according to which part of the tongue is active in their articulation, as <u>front</u>, <u>central</u>, or <u>back</u>. In addition, some English vowels are further distinguished according to whether the tongue is <u>tense</u> or <u>lax</u> in their production. Tense vowels in English are usually pronounced with a /y/-glide (if the vowel is front) or /w/-glide (if the vowel is back). Spanish vowels, however, are relatively pure, and lack these glides. In addition to the simple vowels, there are several diphthongs in English (vowel + glide), notably /ay/, /aw/, and /oy/.

The following are distinctive vowel sounds in most varieties of American English:[2]

		Front	Central	Back
HIGH	(Tense)	/iy/ beet		/uw/ boot
	(Lax)	/ɪ/ bit		/ʊ/ book

---

[2]There are four main regional dialects of American English, each with its own distinctive pronunciation patterns, particularly evident in the vowels. These four dialects are traditionally labeled Northern, North Midland, South Midland, and Southern. For more information, see the bibliography at the end of this section.

		Front	Central	Back
MID	(Tense)	/ey/ bait	/ə/ but	/ow/ boat
	(Lax)	/ɛ/ bet		
LOW		/æ/ bat	/a/ cot	/ɔ/ caught
DIPHTHONGS		/ay/ tie	/aw/ how	/oy/ boy

The most efficient way to predict pronunciation problems for speakers of one language learning another is to compare the phonemic systems of the two languages. We may illustrate some of the procedures involved by predicting problems of phonological interference by comparing the phonemic systems of English and (American) Spanish.

Phonemes of English (consonants)

```
p    t       k
b    d       g
            č
           (ǰ)
f  (θ) s  (š)   h
(v)(ð)(z)(ž)
m    n      (ŋ)
w    l  y    r
```

Phonemes of Spanish (consonants)

```
p    t       k
b    d       g
            č
f    s       x
m    n  ñ
w    l  y    ř
                ř̃
```

Phonemes of English[3] (vowels)

```
(iy)   (uw)
( ɪ)   ( ʊ)

(ey)  (ə)  (ow)
( ɛ)  ( a) ( ɔ)
( æ)
```

Phonemes of Spanish (vowels)

```
i          u

e          o

     a
```

In comparing two such phonemic systems, the first step is to draw a circle around the symbols for phonemes in the target language—which in this case is English—which are absent in the native language.

---

[3] In some dialects of the North and the West Coast, there is no contrast between /a/ and /ɔ/, so that words such as stock and stalk, cot and caught, are pronounced alike. Thus while in these dialects the Spanish speaker will find stalk identical to stock, in other dialects stalk will for him sound like stoke and caught like coat. It will be noted that in the above chart, pairs of vowels have been circled to show how the Spanish speaker hears the vowels within each circle as a single vowel.

If we compare the English and Spanish systems, we find that both of them have /p t č k b d g/, but the /ǰ/ is absent in Spanish; we can predict, then, that English /ǰ/ will be a problem for Spanish speakers (which they will hear as /y/), because it is a new unit in the sound system, one that does not exist in their native system as a separate phoneme.

Continuing our comparison, we find /f/ in both languages, but /θ/ (the initial sound of <u>theta</u>) is not present in American Spanish. Nevertheless, some Spanish speakers may know how Castilians sound, for the /θ/ does exist in the Castilian dialect of Spanish, and they may know how to imitate the sound. However, they will still have perceptual difficulties discriminating /θ/ as a separate phoneme. We note that Spanish has no phonemic contrast, as English does, between /š/ and /č/; it is predictable, then, that Spanish speakers will have trouble hearing and producing the contrast between <u>share</u> and <u>chair</u>, or <u>wash</u> and <u>watch</u>. Spanish has a /x/ (voiceless velar fricative), which English lacks, while English has a /h/ not found in Spanish (it must be remembered at this point that we are talking about speech, not writing). It is normal for the speakers of either language to use their native phoneme (/x/ or /h/) in speaking the other language; in this situation, where one phoneme is simply substituted for another, the result contributes to a foreign "accent" but does not really impede communication. Thus the English speaker who pronounces <u>mujer</u> as /muwhɛr/ and the Spanish speaker who pronounces <u>hot</u> as /xat/ are still intelligible, though their accent is unmistakable.

An entire series of English phonemes, the voiced fricatives /v ð z ž/, are absent from Spanish, so that all of them will pose a learning problem for the Spanish speaker. The problem is complicated by the fact that some of these sounds occur in Spanish phonetically, but not phonemically, hence Spanish speakers will find it difficult to perceive them as distinct sounds. Going on down our chart to the nasals, we find /m/ and /n/ in both languages; Spanish has an /ñ/, which English lacks, so this will pose no problem for the Spanish speaker learning English, to whom this phoneme will merely be "extra baggage", so to speak. English on the other hand, has the phoneme /ŋ/ which does not occur in Spanish as a phoneme. Although both [n] and [ŋ] occur phonetically in Spanish, they never contrast to signal a difference in meaning as they do in English. For Spanish speakers, then, both sounds are members of the same phoneme, whereas in English they belong to different phonemes.

Finally, we find /w y l/ in both languages, but Spanish has /ř/ and /ř̄/, while English has only /r/. In this instance it is the English speaker studying Spanish who must learn to subdivide his /r/-habits into two. We know from considerable experience that the <u>r</u>-problem is one which English speakers have in learning Spanish, and not vice versa.

Comparing the vowels, we see that the vowel system of English is extremely complex. English has one of the most complex systems in the world, which is certainly unfortunate considering its status as a world language. English speakers make phonemic distinctions between /iy, ɪ, ey, ɛ, æ/ among the front vowels, in such words as <u>beet</u>, <u>bit</u>, <u>bait</u>, <u>bet</u>, <u>bat</u>; in the central vowel column we have the distinction between /ə, a/ as in <u>cut</u> and <u>cot</u>; and in the back the differences between /uw, ʊ, ow, ɔ/ are phonemic, as in <u>pool</u>, <u>pull</u>, <u>pole</u>, and <u>pall</u>. While we have all these different vowel distinctions to make in English, the Spanish speaker has only five to worry about. The English speaker learning Spanish finds a much simpler system and so has no real problem aside from the differences in articulatory norms which contribute to an accent. On the other hand, the Spanish speaker learning English has to divide his system of five vowels into eleven vowels of English, which is to say that he must more than double the number of distinctions he makes in his native vowels in order to understand and be understood in English. The size of this learning problem can readily be appreciated. Its further relevance to spelling and reading cannot be emphasized too much, since for the Spanish-speaking child, such words as <u>sheep</u>, <u>ship</u>, <u>cheap</u>, and <u>chip</u> will be heard as alike and will consequently tend to be spelled alike. When a Spanish-speaking child writes <u>these dog</u> or <u>this dogs</u>, he is not making a grammatical mistake (though it may appear so), but for him <u>this</u> and <u>these</u> sound exactly alike, and he has simply forgotten which spelling to use in which situation.

The phonemic system of a language acts as a kind of filter through which the native speaker hears the sounds of other languages. This "phonemic filter" assigns the sounds of foreign languages to the nearest equivalent phoneme in the native language. If the native language lacks /θ/, the student learning English will often fail to hear it as a new sound, but will perceive it as the phonetically most similar sound in his language; e.g., as /t/, /s/, or occasionally as /f/. If the native language has no phonemic distinction between /ə/ and /a/, for example, they will be heard as identical sounds. The perceptual system of the brain automatically pigeon-holes all language sounds (unless they are too novel) into the phonemic categories to which the speaker has been conditioned by his previous language experience.

Some of the problems of phonemic differentiation which the Spanish speaker faces in learning English are listed below. We have previously identified most of these in our initial contrastive analysis of the two phonemic systems, but the mode of presentation adopted here may help to bring these into sharper focus.

38 / A HANDBOOK OF BILINGUAL EDUCATION

Spanish	English
/č/	/č/ chair, watch
	/š/ share, wash
/s/	/s/ sip, racer
	/z/ zip, razor
/n/	/n/ sin
	/ŋ/ sing
/b/	/b/ bat, rabble
	/v/ vat, ravel
/t/	/t/ tin
/s/	/θ/ thin
	/s/ sin
/d/	/d/ den, ladder
	/ð/ then, lather
/y/	/y/ yellow, yet
	/j/ Jello, jet
/i/	/iy/ cheap
	/ɪ/ chip
/e/	/ey/ bait
	/ɛ/ bet
	/æ/ bat
/a/	/ə/ cut
	/a/ cot

THE LANGUAGES OF INSTRUCTION / 39

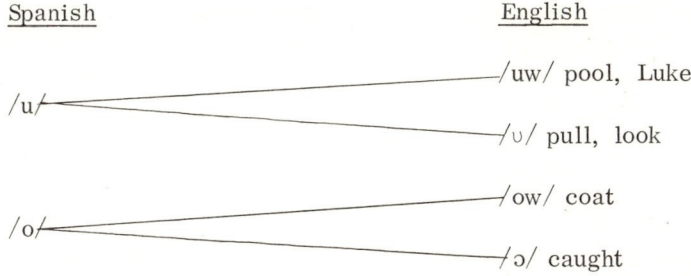

Certain sounds which are phonemically distinct in English are found to occur in Spanish as members of the same phoneme. For example, both of the sounds [d] and [ð] occur in Spanish, where they never contrast and are both members of the phoneme /d/. Their distribution may be illustrated by the following examples:

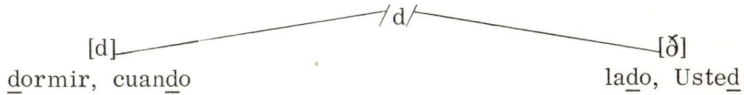

[d]   [ð]
dormir, cuando   lado, Usted

As shown, the stop [d] occurs initially and after nasals while the fricative [ð] occurs between vowels and in final position. Their occurrence is predictable and automatic, and the native speaker of Spanish hears them as phonemically equivalent. As a result, he fails to hear or produce any distinction between such pairs of English words as dare-there, ladder-lather, and read-wreathe.

A similar situation involves the sounds [n] and [ŋ], which in English belong to different phonemes but in Spanish are members of the same phoneme. Their distribution is as follows:

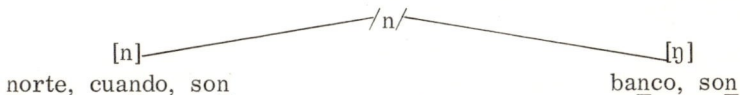

[n]   [ŋ]
norte, cuando, son   banco, son

Words which end in /n/ may be pronounced indifferently either with [n] or [ŋ], though in some dialects there is a greater tendency to use [ŋ] in this position. Before velar stops or fricatives, only [ŋ] is found; [n] occurs in all other positions. Spanish speakers, therefore, have great difficulty detecting any perceptible difference between such English pairs as sin and sing, and even greater difficulty producing such a distinction. Occasionally they are misled by the orthography and actually attempt to pronounce the g in sing, often saying something closer to sink.

In Cuban and Puerto Rican Spanish, /s/ after vowels is often pronounced [h] or dropped altogether. This practice, transferred to English, may produce difficulties with the plural and possessive suffixes on nouns, and the third singular present suffix on verbs.

If the languages of instruction in a bilingual program are English and Navajo, a similar comparison of the phonemic systems would be made.

Phonemes of English

```
 p       t      k
 b       d      g
                č
                ǰ
 f  θ    s  š       h
 v  ð    z  ž
 m       n      ŋ
 w       l  y   r
```

```
iy       uw
ɪ        ʊ
ey   ə   ow
ɛ
æ    a   ɔ
```

Phonemes of Navajo

```
        t    k    k
        tʔ   kʔ        ʔ
   b    d    g
        ts   č    tł
        tsʔ  čʔ   tłʔ
        dz   ǰ    dl
        s    š         h   x
        z    ž             gh
   m    n
   w    l    y
        ł
```

```
   i
             o
   e
   a
```

There are many differences between English and Navajo in the exact pronunciation of sounds which have similar places in the sound systems of the two languages. In this case, Navajo has more consonant distinctions than English, so English speakers have difficulties in perceiving and producing them.

Since there is no distinction between /p/ and /b/ in Navajo, Navajo speakers usually do not distinguish between English /p/ and /b/ and often substitute their own slightly different /b/ for both. Since in Navajo this sound never occurs at the end of a syllable, they often substitute /ʔ/ (a glottal stop) for final /p/ or /b/ or reduce all final stops to the Navajo /d/. This /d/, which sounds like the /t/ in /stæp/, is also typically substituted for English /t/ or /d/ in initial position. The /ʔ/ is frequently substituted for stop consonants and added before initial vowels, making Navajo speech sound choppy to speakers of English. In Navajo there are no sounds which correspond to /f/, /v/, /θ/, /ð/ and /ŋ/, so that all of these constitute learning problems for the Navajo speaker.

The primary differences in the vowel systems are that vowel length and nasalization are used to distinguish meaning in Navajo, and that

English exhibits a greater variety of vowel sounds. The vowels /æ/ and /ə/ do not occur in Navajo and are the hardest for students to learn. Navajo speakers must also learn to distinguish among English /ow/, /ʊ/ and /uw/.

The phonotactics (or distribution of phonemes) of a language should also be considered. English is one of the languages which restricts the occurrence of some phonemes to certain positions, as /h/ to initial and medial word positions (<u>horse</u> and <u>comprehend</u>) and /ž/ to medial and final (<u>azure</u> and <u>rouge</u>). Only certain consonants may cluster in English, and then they occur only in a restricted order. Consonant clusters (blends) present a major problem for students learning English from either a Spanish or Navajo language background. Such combinations as initial /sk/ (as in <u>school</u>) do not occur in Spanish and present a problem to Spanish speakers learning English. Navajo speakers often substitute similar affricates for English consonant clusters. Some of the Navajo's difficulty with noun and verb inflections may be traced to his failure to hear or produce final consonant clusters in English.

Mastery of the sound systems of both languages is essential if misunderstanding is to be avoided. In addition, it is important as a basis for the development of an effective reading program. Complete mastery of new systems of speech sounds is well within the reach of young children, and is a realistic goal of early language instruction if adequate methods are utilized.

Grammar

The grammatical system of a language includes all of the formal features which express meaning or the relationships of elements in sentences. The grammar of one language is different from any other, although some closely related languages have many types of structures in common. English and Spanish will share many more grammatical features than, say, English and Navajo because English and Spanish descend from a common ancestral language (Indo-European), whereas English and Navajo do not.

Traditional school grammars of English are written for use by native speakers, and ignore or take for granted many important features of the language which the nonnative speaker must learn. These traditional school grammars tend to analyze such languages as French, Spanish, and English in a common Latin model, which obscures many of the important differences among these and other languages which need to be taken into account for efficient language instruction. An objective understanding of the unique grammar of the language of instruction is desirable in any classroom; it is essential in bilingual classrooms where contrasting linguistic systems are being used.

Word order is important in many languages. This can be shown in the following sentences, where there is no change in the words themselves, but the difference in the relative <u>order</u> changes the total meaning of the sentences completely:

The boy hit the man.
The man hit the boy.

John is coming.
Is John coming?

We have a guest house.
We have a house guest.

Es mi amigo antiguo.
Es mi antiguo amigo.

The contrast between the word order of Spanish and English may be seen in the following examples:

Es un hombre. (Verb + Noun)
   He is a man. (Noun + Verb + Noun)

Le da el sombrero. (Ind. Obj. + Verb + Dir. Obj.)
   He gives him the hat. (Subj. + Verb + Ind. Obj. + Dir. Obj.)

¿Está abierta la ventana? (Verb + Adj. + Noun)
   Is the window open? (Verb + Noun + Adj.)

This contrast in word order explains why some speakers of Spanish when learning English produce such sentences as <u>Is a man</u>, following the Spanish sentence pattern, or as a question in the Spanish pattern, <u>Is open the window</u>?

The order of elements is less flexible in Navajo than in either English or Spanish, and this order is radically different from that of similar English constructions.

kin íí šłaa 'house, it-I-made'
   (Obj. + Subj. + Verb)

I made a house.
   (Subj. + Verb + Obj.)

tsé šaa yinî'ą 'rock, me-to, it-he-brought'
   (Dir. Obj. + Ind. Obj. + Prep. + Subj. + Verb)

He brought me the rock.
   (Subj. + Verb + Ind. Obj. + Dir. Obj.)

kin bičʔiʔ yišááł   'house, it-toward, along-I-am-walking'
   (Adverb Phrase + Subj. + Verb)

I am walking toward the house.
   (Subj. + Verb + Adverb Phrase)

Most of the inflectional elements of words occur as prefixes in Navajo but as suffixes in English. This may partly explain why Navajo speakers omit inflectional suffixes (such as past tense) in English.

The different word order which is used in different languages is only one reason why word-for-word translations between any two languages is impossible, and helps explain the following nonstandard structures in Spanish in which the speakers were carrying over literal translations from English:

Mi papá's carro for El carro de mi papá.

Lo veo en los sábados for Lo veo los sábados.

¿Han mirado a Luis? for ¿Han visto a Luis?

A vexing grammatical problem which faces the Spanish speaker is the use of <u>in</u>, <u>on</u>, and <u>at</u> in English. The problem exists because Spanish has only one preposition, <u>en</u>, corresponding to all three English prepositions in different contexts. This interference accounts for sentences such as the following in the speech of Spanish-speaking students learning English:

Put the apple <u>in</u> the table.
I live <u>in</u> Durango Street.
I live <u>on</u> 136 Leon Street.

English <u>prepositions</u> may also constitute a potential problem in word order for the Navajo speaker, since they usually correspond to the <u>postpositions</u> of his language. These generally occur as suffixes, very different from English prepositions which precede nouns and are considered separate words. The English phrase <u>toward it</u> would be expressed as bichʔiʔ (bi- 'it', -chʔiʔ 'toward') in Navajo.

Spanish speakers experience some difficulty with the <u>his/her</u> distinction, since both may be expressed by <u>su</u> in Spanish. Navajo speakers find English pronouns a major problem, as do Chinese speakers, since there is no distinction in these languages between subject and object forms such as I/me, he/him, we/us (just as there is none in English for you and it). In addition, Navajo uses a single pronoun, bí, for all third person situations, so that such English distinctions as he/she/it/they, as well as the possessive and objective forms, must be carefully taught. Speakers of both Spanish and Navajo have difficulty with English articles. There are no words in Navajo which correspond exactly to the English definite and indefinite articles (although there are forms which can be used to show definiteness and indefiniteness). Navajo speakers may therefore omit the articles in English, producing such nonstandard constructions as Joe has red hat or Book on table is red. Spanish speakers may omit the indefinite article in places where it is omitted in Spanish, such as before nouns denoting professions: That man is fireman or She's teacher. Indefinite articles may be used incorrectly before mass nouns, as in He has a chalk. In addition, Spanish uses articles instead of possessive pronouns before body-part terms, saying Me lavé las manos 'I washed the hands', instead of 'I washed my hands'.

Both English and Spanish inflect nouns for plurality, but with only a few exceptions, nouns in Navajo do not change form to express singular or plural. Instead, only the verb changes form. Navajo speakers may carry this pattern into English and say something like The horse are running instead of The horses are running.

In English, certain distinctive patterns of variation in the pitch of the voice (intonation) used while uttering a sentence are important in signaling grammatical information, and stress is also extremely important as it functions on several different levels to differentiate words, phrases, and sentences (pérfect (Adj.) vs. perféct (Verb)). It is important to realize that our writing system does not ordinarily indicate the placement of stress, so that we have to know where the stress falls in order to read a sentence appropriately. Punctuation is only an imperfect and partial representation of English intonation patterns. Speakers of other languages find English stress and intonation patterns very difficult to master, and have particular trouble with reading because of the lack of marking in writing, which masks the distinctions of speech.

The Spanish intonational system has one less degree of stress than English, different stress and rhythmical patterns, and different intonational contours. A speaker of Spanish is likely to give every syllable a nearly equal length of time, to shorten English stressed syllables, to put stress on the wrong syllable, and to fail to reduce vowels to /ə/ in unstressed syllables. (Of course English speakers learning Spanish have all of these problems in reverse.)

Navajo uses pitch differences to signal different words, whereas English never uses pitch for this purpose. On the other hand, English sometimes makes use of stress to distinguish meaning in words, as mentioned above, whereas stress is never distinctive in Navajo. Consequently Navajo speakers may experience difficulty in perceiving the stress differences on English words, just as English speakers have trouble perceiving the tone differences in Navajo.

Particles are used in Navajo to convey meanings expressed by intonation in English. For instance, daʔ-íš and -ša added to Navajo words signal questions, -gaʔ gives emphasis, and -ʔas indicates disbelief. Navajo students speak and read English without the appropriate modulations and inflections because they are unaccustomed to the use of intonation to express meaning in these situations. A great deal of drilling on the intonation patterns of different types of sentences is necessary if students are to learn to handle them naturally.

Lexicon

The third major system within language to be considered is the lexicon. This includes more than what we usually call vocabulary: it also includes the cultural referents which words reflect in each language (their meaning), restrictions placed on the selection of words in specific contexts, and an analysis of which words may occur together in a language and which may not.

A lexical system is essentially a linguistic organization of experience. This organization is not exactly the same for speakers of any two languages, and apparent meaning equivalents in more than one language are often misleading. All too often, as students learn new words in the second language they try to superimpose on them the same categories into which experiences are classified in the native language. The different classification of colors in Navajo and English was mentioned above; the Navajo speaker uses the term dootł'ʔizh to refer to the range of the spectrum divided by English speakers into green and blue. This does not mean the speakers of both languages can't perceive the same gradations in color; the only difference is categorization, and it can be expressed when necessary. When a Navajo speaker needs to express green as opposed to blue, for instance, he calls it tátł'ʔid naxalingo dootł'ʔizh 'blue/green like algae'.

Because cultures are reflected so vividly in the lexicons of languages, learning a second language requires learning new patterns of thought. An English speaker is used to thinking of legs and back and neck as belonging to all animate creatures, as well as to some inanimate objects such as chairs. When learning Spanish, that speaker must learn to consider animals in a different category from humans, with patas, lomo, and pescuezo instead of piernas, espaldo, and cuello.

Western European languages contain a concept of compulsion and obligation which must be learned by Navajos to express such ideas in English as cause, force, compel, make, order, have to, etc. Navajo lacks means for expressing such concepts strongly in language; there are causative verb forms, but these only occur with inanimate objects. English speakers learning Navajo may find that they just cannot express the idea they have if they want to say I have to do that now.

Many other differences in premises and basic categories can be illustrated in the differences between the Navajo and English languages. English rough is perceived as different attributes with different labels (dighol, digóón, and dichʔíízh) depending on whether it is seen as the texture of a road, a rock, or a file, but the last category (dichʔíízh) includes the 'rough' texture of both a file and a pimply face. The single category in Navajo labeled béésh includes English flint, metal, and knife. A Navajo speaker learning English must learn to make a verbal distinction among different types of rough surface.

No appeal to logic will solve the problems in translation that occur because there are not exactly equivalent terms in two languages. The Spanish-speaker, for instance, has no exact translation for bowl, or the word he may use (e. g. cajete) covers a much wider range than English bowl. It is fallacious for teachers lacking cross-linguistic knowledge to assume that a label in English "naturally" expresses a single concept. The child who knows esquina and rincón may have trouble seeing corner as a "concept", as the English-speaking child may have trouble remembering different words for different contexts. Spanish-speakers must learn separate words in English for nuñeca (wrist and doll), abrigar (to protect and to warm), and dedo (finger and toe).

Kinship terminology gives us another example of the different cultural categorizations reflected in language. Navajo sizaani is often the equivalent of my wife, but also may include mother, sister, or any grown woman in the household. A mother's sister's children (cousins in English) are classified as brothers and sisters, but a mother's brother's children are not. Some distinctions are made in Navajo kinship terms that are not made in English: older brother has a different verbal form than younger brother (šíai vs. sitsíli); grandchildren are distinguished as šináli 'son's children' and sitsúi 'daughter's children'. The Spanish compadre relationship between parents and godparents also lacks a single term in English.

Another type of lexical problem is the different distribution of words in languages. Water in English, for instance, can occur in glass of water, water the flowers, and water meter, but Spanish agua can occur only as a noun (unless its form is changed).

Every child learns a great deal of his language from his peer group. A child learns the subtle nuances of meanings of words by trial and error testing against other members of his group in actual communication. By the time he enters school, the child knows most of the language he feels a need for in order to communicate with other members of his own group about everything in his culture which is important to him. The educational program must give him reasons to know more language if it is to teach him more successfully.

Speakers of each language view reality in terms of different cultural and psychological frameworks. This allows economy, because the framework allows speakers to perceive only what is relevant and to organize the perceptions in culturally meaningful ways. Learning a second language involves learning a new cultural framework, and new ways of relating linguistically to members of another social group. This, too, seems to be a capacity often lost after puberty, but readily available to children in bilingual education programs if both languages are taught in meaningful situations and through the contexts of the cultures in which the languages are spoken.

SELECTED BIBLIOGRAPHY

Fishman, Joshua A. 1969. The multiple prediction of phonological variables in a bilingual speech community. American anthropologist 71, 4.

Francis, W. Nelson. 1958. The structure of American English. New York, Ronald Press. (Especially Chapters 2-3 on phonetics and phonemics and Chapter 9 on dialects.)

Hammer, John H. and Frank A. Rice. 1965. A bibliography of contrastive linguistics. Washington, D.C., Center for Applied Linguistics.

The invisible minority. 1966. Report of the NEA-Tucson survey on the teaching of Spanish to the Spanish-speaking. Washington, D.C., NEA, Department of Rural Education.

Kluckhohn, Clyde and Dorothea Leighton. 1960. The Navaho. Cambridge, Harvard University Press.

Lado, Robert. 1957. Linguistics across cultures. Ann Arbor, The University of Michigan Press.

Lance, Donald M. 1969. A brief study of Spanish-English bilingualism. College Station, Texas, Texas A & M University. ERIC No. ED 032 529.

The linguistic reporter. Newsletter of the Center for Applied Linguistics, 1717 Massachusetts Avenue, N.W., Washington, D.C. 20036. Subscription rate $1.50 per year.

Stockwell, Robert P., J. Donald Bowen, and John W. Martin. 1965. The grammatical structures of English and Spanish. Chicago, Illinois, The University of Chicago Press.

Troike, Rudolph C. Forthcoming. Introduction to English linguistics for the teacher of English. New York, McGraw-Hill. (See Chapter 3 on phonology and Chapter 4 on dialectology.)

Vallejo, Bernardo. 1970. La distribucion y estratificacion de /r/ /r̄/ y /s/ en el Español Cubano. Austin, Texas, The University of Texas (doctoral dissertation).

Venezky, Richard L. 1967. English orthography—its graphical structure and its relation to sound. Reading research quarterly, spring. ERIC No. ED 014 410.

Young, Robert W. 1967. English as a second language for Navajos. Albuquerque Area Office, Department of the Interior, Bureau of Indian Affairs.

CHAPTER V

PEDAGOGICAL CONSIDERATIONS

Introduction

Teachers new to bilingual programs often feel unsure of what pedagogical techniques and materials to use in their classrooms—even when they have had many years of successful teaching experience. Some of the procedures suggested here are new and must be tried before confidence is established with them. Some of the procedures are based on traditional axioms in education and have merely been adapted to bilingual education. The following are suggestions from both categories which should be considered fundamental to any bilingual program:

- accept the child where he is and build upon his previously acquired capabilities. Each child will bring a large variety of concepts to school, and at least one language complete with sound system, grammar and vocabulary.
- while there will still be aspects of the child's native language that he needs to learn, you are not just teaching him more about his language. You are using his dominant language to teach him other things.
- a second language is not "caught" by mere exposure. Effective and efficient second-language teaching requires a sequential and systematic presentation of structural elements with students of all ages.
- where the child's native dialect differs in some respect from the standard ("classroom") form of the language, effort should be made to avoid stigmatizing the child's native forms. Second language-teaching techniques can be used to help the child develop fluent control over the classroom dialect.
- the construction or selection of instructional materials and evaluative measures should be based where possible on a contrastive analysis of the native and target languages.
- direct instruction in two languages should be at different periods of the day to discourage translation-type learning.

provision should always be made for different rates of learning and different levels of experience, interest, and attention span.

children need many chances to practice understanding and speaking in different types of meaningful situations. Even language drills should have meaning.

learning a new language involves learning a new skill, acquiring a new set of habits. Incorrect responses should be minimized and corrected by having the student repeat after the teacher-model. Children enjoy the disciplined kind of activity involved in language drills, which are essential for the reinforcement of new linguistic habits.

a child's success in learning a new language will be largely dependent on his need to know it. His motivation is a crucial component and should not be neglected.

The curriculum

The bilingual curriculum includes four basic content areas: communication, environmental concepts and relationships, creative expression, and abstract concept development. Communication involves understanding and producing two languages, and the later development of reading and writing skills; environmental concepts and relationships includes the study of social and physical surroundings; creative expression includes both art and music; and abstract concept development includes mathematical concepts, such abstractions as "same" and "different", and the knowledge of letter names.

Initial success in reading is perhaps the single most important goal in primary education, since reading forms the basis for much of subsequent education. One of the chief weaknesses of monolingual educational programs is that they do not allow a child to begin reading in the language in which he has developed oral competence—unless this happens to be English. The child should begin reading in his dominant language. The child who learns to read first in Spanish or Navajo may have, in fact, a definite advantage over the child who must learn first in English. The writing system of English is not regular, and children must learn that a single sound may be spelled in many different ways. The writing system of Spanish and that which has been developed for Navajo are very regular, with close correspondences between sounds and letters. The child's ability to recognize the relationship between sound and symbol is a major factor in his success in initial reading instruction. The child who learns to read his native language before reading English will not be learning to read twice. The basic skills of reading transfer readily from one language to another. He will, indeed, become literate in two languages, and this is an advantage which might be denied if he began only in English.

Social studies and science concepts can be developed most rapidly in the dominant language of the child, although greater flexibility is possible in this area of the curriculum. Concepts may be developed through the native language and then reinforced in the second language, or the language of the home may be used to study topics related to the home and community and English used for discussing the school environment. The availability of instructional material in each language will influence this linguistic division.

Art and music are areas in which the cultures in the community can most readily be brought into the classroom, and both languages may be used at different times. It is important to help a child understand and respect his own cultural heritage as part of the development of his self-image and self-concept. In addition, understanding the cultural heritage of others in the community will help deter the formation of negative stereotypes and prejudice.

Computational skills should be developed in English, as explained in the design section above. Students continue to perform basic mathematical processes in the language in which they first learned them, and more advanced courses in mathematics will probably require the use of English.

Oral language is undoubtedly the most pervasive component of any educational program in the primary grades, and special consideration is given below to techniques for effective second-language instruction.

Language teaching

Various methods of teaching language have been suggested and tried at all levels of instruction and with various degrees of success. Particularly in the primary grades, an emphasis has often been placed on "fostering attitudes" and "developing interests", accompanied by little or no direct language instruction. Some have felt that children "catch" a second language by exposure, much as they catch the measles, but this has not proved to be the case. Others have placed an emphasis on learning vocabulary lists without regard to the sounds or structure of the language. Still others have added a year of instruction, usually a pre-first, which ranges from a year of concentrated language study with specially prepared teachers and materials to a year of unstructured activity during which the children are only expected to grow older. Some improvements have been reported in the academic achievement of students in the special language classes, but there are social disadvantages inherent in any program which segregates children with different native languages. The extra year of instruction, even when linguistically beneficial, in fact retards the children chronologically in school and may make subsequent behavior problems and dropouts more likely. These disadvantages may be outweighed by other gains, but the search for more effective methods has continued.

The methods suggested in this guide try to set a pattern of success for the children in language learning. They do not require "trial and error" learning, or random activity with haphazard or selective reinforcement. Children should be asked to produce only what they first understand, and opportunities for mistakes should be minimized.

The immediate goals of second-language instruction are to have the children be able to discriminate and produce the distinctive sounds (phonemes) of the target language in the context of words (never in isolation), to interpret and produce its basic sentence patterns, and to use an adequate vocabulary.

An important concept in language teaching is focus. When new elements of vocabulary, structures, or pronunciation are being introduced, it should be in the context of elements which have been taught previously. For example, if new vocabulary items are being introduced, they should be presented in sentence patterns which are already familiar so that students will be able to focus on the new items without any distraction or confusion from the grammatical structure. If an unfamiliar grammatical feature is introduced at the same time, it will destroy the focus on the vocabulary. Phonology drills often necessarily require new vocabulary items, but familiar words should be used as much as possible. A grammatical drill should not contain new vocabulary items, and to be effective, should contain as little switching of vocabulary as possible from sentence to sentence. The following excerpt from a substitution drill on possessive pronouns will illustrate the point:

Teacher: This is <u>John's</u> book. (<u>his</u>)
Students: This is <u>his</u> book.
Teacher: This is <u>Bill's</u> book. (<u>his</u>)
Students: This is <u>his</u> book.

Each point should be focused on and drilled adequately before a new point is taken up. For example, a number of substitutions using <u>his</u> should be given before switching to <u>her</u>. Alternative forms (e.g. different pronouns, verb tenses, types of noun plurals) should not be intermixed until each has been practiced separately. Consistency in the presentation as well as in the organization of drills is important if the practice which they provide is to be effective.

It is more desirable to teach the full forms of language before the reduced forms. To be sure, people are more likely to say <u>He's coming</u> than <u>He is coming</u>. But the purpose of language teaching is to teach systems which speakers can manipulate to create new forms. Having

PEDAGOGICAL CONSIDERATIONS / 53

learned the full form, (He is coming) the child can easily go on to learn both the contraction and the question and negative constructions, Is he coming, and He isn't coming. If, on the other hand, he has learned the contracted form first, it may not be readily obvious to him how to derive questions and negatives from it. At a later time, he will learn that full forms are appropriate to more formal contexts, while contractions are appropriate in informal situations.

When the structural framework has been learned using a limited number of words, the required vocabulary can easily be added. This is not to suggest that the vocabulary is not important; the question is only one of initial emphasis and perspective.

The elements of language are best taught in the following order: listening, speaking, reading, writing. Children should first hear the language before they are required to produce what they have heard. Reading and writing come only after some fluency has been achieved in speech, and even then, the initial written material should contain no structures which have not first been introduced orally. In a fully bilingual program, all children will be taught in two languages. Instruction in two languages, however, should usually be at different times of the day to discourage translation-type learning and to minimize interference between the languages.

Similar vocabulary items may be presented through the structures of both languages, although lexical equivalence is not necessarily desirable. Function words will be needed in both languages, and the content words should be selected for immediate need and usefulness in each language. Motivation to learn words is higher when they are needed, and when there is occasion to use them repeatedly, their retention is more likely. Good sources for the vocabulary content of language drills are the texts for other subject areas and other basic words relating to home, family, and school. In all activities and experiences in the curriculum, emphasis should be placed on developing the concepts for which labels can be provided in both languages of instruction.

At the very outset of any bilingual education program, in fact from the very first day, children should be taught certain basic classroom instructions in the second language, so that these can be used by the teacher thereafter for effective classroom control. In addition, children can be taught certain fixed phrases, such as greeting forms, appropriate question forms for asking permission to do certain things, etc. These functional elements can and should be taught independently from the regular curricular sequence of language structures, since they will be largely fixed and invariable.

Practical teaching suggestions

1. The optimum size group for direct language instruction is 8-10; probably no more than 12 students should ever be placed in a single

group for most language-teaching activities. Above this point the teacher cannot maintain close enough contact with students, and most important, there will not be enough time for individual practice. Small groups allow maximum time for individual practice and for the teacher to monitor individual problems and correct errors before students have a chance to practice them.

2. If possible, students should be arranged in a semicircle for language instruction, so that their attention will be focused on the teacher and so the teacher will be able to maintain better contact and class control. In addition, this arrangement facilitates student interaction in communicative activities. Rows and columns of chairs are inimical to effective language teaching.

3. Students should not be called in a particular order, but the teacher should skip around the group to hold their attention. For the same reason, a child should not be called on until after a question has been asked or directions given. If a child knows he will not be called on, he is likely not to listen further.

4. The pace of language drills is very important. A brisk tempo should be maintained at all times to keep students' interest and attention. Boredom quickly sets in if a drill is too slow.

5. Real objects should be used whenever possible to illustrate meaning. Pictures are also helpful, but a variety should be used to help define the range of experience covered by the word. Illustrations of a chair, for instance, should include armchairs, wooden chairs, and several varieties called "chair" in English. Pictures should be large enough for the children to see easily.

6. The teacher should not attempt to teach students a phonemic distinction she does not make in her native dialect. Depending on the part of the country she comes from, the teacher may not differentiate, for instance, between cot and caught, pin and pen, or witch and which. Even if the teacher has succeeded in mastering such distinctions for drill purposes, she will probably return to her normal usage in context. If she attempts to "fake" her pronunciation, students will often quickly recognize the inconsistency, and her teaching effectiveness will be reduced.

7. Language teaching is not something which goes on just during the scheduled language period. A wide variety of activities during the day should be used to reinforce patterns which have been introduced in that period. Lining up for recess, for instance, invites a "chain drill" for the production of /č/ in which the teacher says "I choose ____," that child says "I choose ____," and so on until all the children are in line. During P. E. a relay game may be organized in which each student bounces a ball to the next in line saying "Bounce the volley ball." This drill is useful for the /b-v/ distinction, often difficult for speakers of Spanish.

8. Language drills in game form can be available for the students whenever they have free time to choose an activity. Pictures may be grouped on a flannel board or pasted in a scrapbook, for instance, sorted according to which words begin with the same sound.

9. Slides of field trips and special school functions provide good bilingual language activities when the students prepare taped "sound tracks" in two languages and show them to other classes, PTA, or at open house activities.

10. Much of the motivation for learning language comes when that language is needed to communicate. The teacher can foster this by heterogeneous assignment of students to classes, and by seating arrangements and grouping within the classroom which create the opportunity and need for students of varied language backgrounds to talk to each other.

11. Extra drill is needed on irregular items (such as forms of be) and items involving interference between the native and target languages. This is the reason material prepared for one language is not necessarily applicable to other language groups. The present progressive is not a problem for speakers of Spanish, but is for speakers of Navajo. The whole point of contrastive analysis is to determine what to teach and how much time to devote to the various linguistic features so identified.

Phonology

Very early in the program, the phonemic contrasts which exist in one language, but not the other, should be taught. The concepts "same-different" need to be understood before they can be applied to the sounds of language. These concepts, as used in the development of both visual and auditory discrimination skills, are taught in most reading readiness programs. Because understanding them is a necessary prerequisite for language drills, the concepts "same-different" should be presented during the first week of school. The following activities may be used to introduce these concepts at the kindergarten or first grade level:

Have several noise-makers in front of the class and show and ring two at a time. "These sounds are the same" (ring two cowbells). "These sounds are different" (ring a cowbell and a triangle). At this stage the children can also see that the noise-makers are different. After the concept "same-different" is understood, the objects can be hidden in a bag or box and the children asked to determine "the same" or "different" on the basis of sound alone.

Small items, such as beans, cotton, seeds, or buttons, can be put in pill bottles covered with adhesive paper. The children may take turns shaking two bottles and deciding if they are "the same" or "different". They may look inside to check their answers.

The children who are able to do this activity are ready to begin the discrimination of speech sounds.

Learning the sounds of a language begins with ear training—with hearing the significant differences (i.e., which are considered "the same" and which are considered "different" by native speakers of that language). Children find it very easy to imitate speech sounds, but successful mimicry by no means assures that they will produce the sound in other words or at other times when it is appropriate. Many teachers have been disheartened after a language lesson stressing the ch sound in English for speakers of Spanish when the children are again sitting on *shairs, waving hands at the *teasher for a chance to *shoose the next activity. The non-English occurs because the children, although they can produce both sh and ch, may not have realized the significance of the difference between them, or may not have had enough practice distinguishing the sounds both in hearing and in speaking. Successful mastery of any skill takes time. A good teacher knows that one lesson is not enough to establish a concept or skill in most students. There is thus a need for continued drill while habits are firmly established and transferred to free production.

Language drills can be organized into play activities or meaningful communication exchanges. The following examples illustrate drills for promoting the /š-č/ distinction, but similar activities can be applied to other pairs of sounds.

Make a chart with two pockets and several 3x6 flash cards of pictures illustrating words containing /š/ and /č/. One picture for each sound should be pasted over the pockets. Children sort the flash cards into the appropriate pockets.

Say several words containing both /š/ and /č/. Children clap softly only when they hear /š/. Say the list again with the children clapping when they hear /č/.

Discrimination activities should be continued in the curriculum until all students show satisfactory performance. After each phoneme can be heard as distinct from other similar phonemes with which it is apt to be confused, activities to teach its production will be much more effective. The children's responses may be made by the entire class, small groups, or individuals. Children are usually more willing to speak out as part of a group than they are alone in a new situation, and their attention is likely to be lost if they have to wait for too many others to have a turn. Group practice increases the amount of practice for each individual, but one problem is that it is difficult for the teacher to hear if individuals are pronouncing sounds correctly. Group responses can be somewhat chaotic if the children are speaking at a slightly different time. The teacher should develop a repertory of hand signals and use them consistently to let the children know at which times to listen and exactly when to speak as a group or individually.

During group response, it helps for the teacher to move around and "tune in" different individuals, to check on their pronunciation. If a child is making a mistake the teacher can switch to individual drill to help the child, then switch back to group work. The teacher needs to become sensitive to how long to prolong group or individual drill and when to switch from one to another. Probably no drill should be entirely group or individual. Alternating the two types helps provide variety. The following are examples of different types of responses:

Cut small shoes from colored paper. Put them in a box or bag and have a child close his eyes and choose a shoe. The others say:
   New shoes, new shoes,
   Which color do you choose?
The individual child says:
   I choose (color) shoes.
If the child has the color he chose, he gets another turn. If not, he loses his turn to the next player.

Have pictures of food. The children take turns choosing something for lunch. Each says, "I choose ____ for my lunch."

Have a number of sea shells, or pictures of them, on a table. Let the children take turns getting a shell and putting it on a chair, saying "I put my shell on the chair." This could be played as a relay. Have two lines of children and see which line finishes first.

Notice that even when concentrating on teaching sounds of a language, these are not presented or practiced in isolation. Speech sounds occur as parts of words, and words as parts of sentences. Language is a way of conveying meaning, and this essential characteristic should not be left out of language lessons. Individual phonemes can be isolated by using words which are minimal pairs—words which are identical except for the sound you want to call attention to. These can be introduced in the following way:

Say minimal pairs, illustrated with pictures or actions or explained in the native language whenever possible, and have the children repeat them. It is important at all times that the children know the meaning of the words.

chair	share
choose	shoes
chew	shoe
watching	washing
chip	ship
cheap	sheep
catch	cash
match	mash
ditch	dish

Say pairs of words and ask if they are "the same" or "different".

chair	chair
shoe	shoe
chip	ship

After the children can hear which are the same and which are different, say one of each pair and have a child respond by pointing to the appropriate picture, making the correct action, or giving the correct native-language equivalent.

Once these distinctions can be heard, the words may be included in minimal pair sentences. In this way, even though the focus of the drill is on phonology, syntactic fluency will be reinforced through practice on sentence patterns. Again make sure the children know the meaning of the other words in the sentence; otherwise the focus will be lost.

Say the following pairs of sentences and have the children act out the appropriate one or identify the appropriate picture.

I have a chip.
I have a ship.

I'm watching dishes.
I'm washing dishes.

After the children understand what sound you want them to be listening for, more varied activities can be used:

Put pictures containing /š/ and /č/ face down on a table and let the children pretend to go shopping for these items. One child picks up a picture, shows it to the class and says, "I am shopping for a ____" (saying whatever is on the card). After all the pictures have been turned face up, children who did not have a turn shopping find one they like and say "I choose the ____." They then tell the class something about it.

Syntax

The grammatical structure of a language cannot be taught without using words, nor words without using speech sounds. Therefore, although in teaching we focus on one new element at a time to avoid confusion, the teaching of phonology, syntax, and vocabulary should be an integrated process. The rate of instruction should remain flexible, and no definite limits set as to what structures must be covered in every classroom each day. Once a particular sequence of situations is chosen, however, it should be followed consistently. Language learning is cumulative; new structures build on what has already been learned. In addition, the material is graded, with easier structures presented first so that several new features are not introduced at the same time.

This cumulative development is analogous to the "stages" a child goes through in his physical development; he must learn to walk before he can run, and to run before he can perform the more complicated physical task of skipping. Just as normal children progress through these stages at varying rates, so they may be expected to progress at different rates through the stages of learning a second language. While walking seems to require conscious effort on the part of a very young child who is just learning the skill, it becomes an automatic habit which he continues to practice even after he has learned more demanding skills. Language skills, too, become habits, and the basic structures which are learned very early will continue in frequent use even when more complicated ones are added.

Each language lesson should contain a variety of structured activities. Some of the basic types of pattern practices are illustrated below:

Mim-Mem—mimicry-memorization. Children imitate a model and then repeat until the response is memorized.

> Hold up pictures of an airplane, rabbit, hat, kitten, cowboy, and horse (or any other six count nouns), and say with each:
>   This is a ____.
> As you say each sentence, stress the intonation pattern, not by explanation, but by example.
> Give each child a smaller picture of each object. One at a time, the children hold up one of their flash cards and say:

This is a _____.
Have the children repeat after you as a group and individually. If any child does not use the correct intonation pattern (lets his voice rise at the end of the statement or pitches "this" higher than the noun), correct him by repeating his response and slightly exaggerating the proper intonation pattern.

<u>Chain-drill</u>—one child makes a statement or response, then another child, and then another.

Choose one child to be "it". Give him a thimble (or any other article containing /θ/). He says "Thank you for the thimble." He chooses a child and passes the thimble on to him. The game continues until each child has had a chance to say, "Thank you for the thimble."

Choose one child to start a winking game. He is to wink at a friend and say, "I am winking at Mary." Mary turns toward someone else and says, "I am winking at _____."

<u>Substitution</u>—a word is replaced by another word of the same grammatical class, as a noun for a noun.

Put three pictures on a table or other support several feet away and hold three in front of the children. Alternate describing the pictures, saying "This is a _____; that is a _____." One at a time, have the children hold up smaller pictures of the same objects and say, "This is a _____." The children should then point to the picture held by the teacher and say, "That is a _____."

<u>Replacement</u>—replace one element by another, as a pronoun for a noun.

Distribute pictures or objects to all of the children. Ask, "Who has the _____?" The child who has it holds it in the air and all respond, "(Mary) has the _____." Then you ask "What does (Mary) have?" The children again respond "She has the _____."

<u>Conversion</u>—replace one form of a word with another, as past for present progressive.

Teacher: He <u>is looking</u> at a book.
Students: He <u>looked</u> at a book.

PEDAGOGICAL CONSIDERATIONS / 61

<u>Expansion</u>—give the children a word to be added to a sentence.

> Distribute pictures of a big pony, a little pony, and a fast pony. Say only one word, the adjective. If it is "fast", the child with the fast pony holds it up and responds "This is the fast pony."

<u>Transformation</u>—change in word order, as from statement to question, or positive statement to negative statement.

> Let one of the children hide one of the vocabulary pictures and act out the word it represents. The other children guess, "Is that a ____?" The child who is "it" responds "Yes, it is a ____" or "No, it is not a ____." The first child to guess correctly acts out one of his pictures.

Transformation drills can of course be used as chain (AB-BA) drills, as where—one child asks a question, another answers and asks a third, who answers and asks another.

> Ask one child a question, such as, "Can you hop?" He replies, "Yes, I can hop," and hops in front of the class. Then he asks another child, "Can you run?" and the game is repeated with such action words as jump, sit, skip, sing, or any others the children know.

> Pass out small pieces of yarn of different colors and include one piece of yellow. The children close their hands with the yarn as for "Button, Button, Who Has the Button?" Whoever is "it" goes from child to child saying, "Do you have the yellow yarn?" The child questioned should answer, "I don't have the yellow yarn." He then shows his yarn. The child with the yellow yarn says when asked, "I have the yellow yarn." He is then "it".

The following is a partial list of grammatical structures which must be mastered by students learning English as a second language. This list is not intended to say anything about the order of presentation, but only to indicate some of the major structures which need to be included.

>   Verbs
>   present progressive
>   past
>   future

irregular past tense forms
negative forms (<u>don't</u>, <u>won't</u>, <u>isn't</u>, <u>can't</u>, etc.)

Nouns
  proper
  common
    pluralizable (count)
    nonpluralizable (mass)
  irregular plural forms
  pronouns (subj., obj., and poss. forms)

Articles
  (include modifying words such as <u>some</u>, <u>few</u>, <u>any</u>)
  use with mass and count nouns
  demonstratives (agreement with plural nouns)

Adjectives
  comparative and superlative forms

Adverbs
Prepositions
Conjunctions
  <u>and</u>, <u>or</u> (between nouns and between sentences)

Sentence patterns
  N be Adj
  N be N
  N be Adv (place or time)
  N V (Adv)   (intransitive verb pattern)
  N V N (Adv)   (transitive verb pattern)
  Imperative
  Yes, No questions
  Question word questions (<u>who</u>, <u>which</u>, <u>why</u>, <u>how</u>, <u>where</u>)

Vocabulary

    The third major element of language to be considered is vocabulary. The most important words to include in early English lessons are the function words needed to express relationships in the basic sentence patterns. These include articles, prepositions, conjunctions, auxiliaries, interrogatives, and modals.
    The first content words should be those most needed by the children. This criterion for selection will guarantee student motivation for learning the words, and repeated opportunities to use them, maximizing the

probabilities of retention. Topics need not be those closest to the child's experience. The language of the home is usually the one which will be used to talk about the home and family in any case—not English.

When new nouns are introduced, a variety of objects should be used to illustrate the range of meaning whenever possible. Although several nouns are usually taught first in structures like "This is a ____," it is possible that action verbs should be the first content words introduced to young children. This ordering, i.e., learning action words first, permits active responses on the part of the children and actual demonstrations of meaning in both presentation by the teacher and response.

In all language activities, there should be an emphasis on understanding the meaning of what is said and done. Consequently, for the sake of efficiency and understanding, the teacher should be prepared to translate where necessary and when possible.

Reading

Basal reading texts which have been prepared for native English-speaking children are not appropriate for teaching reading to children learning English as a second language. Although vocabularies in readers are carefully controlled, there is seldom any attempt to control the presentation of sentence structures. This is because a child acquires the basic syntactic forms of his first language by the time he is five or six; the complex of syntactic patterns will be a part of his oral language competence before he begins to read. Reading material in a second language needs to grade and control sentence structures as well as vocabulary, and should take into account varying interest levels and experiential backgrounds of the children in the selection of content.

Caution should also be used in the selection of reading material in the child's native language, and local dialect terms and pronunciation checked beforehand. This is especially important for a language as widespread as Spanish, which has important lexical differences among its many regional and national standard dialects. For example, people mow _zacate_ in Mexico, _yerba_ in Cuba, and _grama_ in Puerto Rico, and children fly a _papalote_ in Mexico, _cometa_ in Cuba, and _chiringa_ in Puerto Rico.[1]

Appropriate lexical items and content for initial reading instruction may be found in the stories of the children themselves, and the folklore of a community provides a rich source for reading materials at all levels. Whether using experience charts, folklore, or appropriate pub-

---

[1] Extensive examples of such lexical variations have been collected by Ricardo Cornejo of the Southwest Educational Development Laboratory in Austin, Texas.

lished material, the teacher should always begin with the vocabulary of the child's native dialect and add other dialect terms, or "book" terms, as reading instruction progresses.

SELECTED BIBLIOGRAPHY

Finocchiaro, Mary. 1964. English as a second language: from theory to practice. New York, Simon & Schuster.
_____. 1969. Teaching English as a second language (revised edition). New York, Harper & Row.
Ohannessian, Sirarpi and Dorothy A. Pedtke. 1967. Selected list of materials for teachers of English to speakers of other languages. Washington, D.C., Center for Applied Linguistics. ERIC No. ED 019 675.
_____, et al. 1964. Reference list of materials for English as a second language. Part I—texts, readers, dictionaries, tests. Washington, D.C., Center for Applied Linguistics. ERIC No. ED 014 723.
_____, et al. 1966. Reference list of materials for English as a second language. Part II—background materials, methodology. Washington, D.C., Center for Applied Linguistics. ERIC No. ED 014 724.
Pedtke, Dorothy A., et al. 1969. Reference list of materials for English as a second language. Supplement: 1964-1968. Washington, D.C., Center for Applied Linguistics. ERIC No. ED 025 773.
Prator, Clifford. 1960. A manual of American English pronunciation. New York, Holt, Rinehart and Winston.
Saville, Muriel R. 1969. Curriculum guide for teachers of English in kindergartens for Navajo children. Washington, D.C., Center for Applied Linguistics. ERIC No. ED 030 122.
_____. 1970. Diné bíʔólta saad naaki yeeyáɬtiʔii binaaltsoos tʔááɬáʔígíí (Navajo-English curriculum guide, kindergarten level). Window Rock, Arizona, Bureau of Indian Affairs, Navajo Area Office.
University of Michigan. Bilingual curriculum development. Ann Arbor, Michigan, Ann Arbor Board of Education; Center for Research on Language and Language Behavior, University of Michigan.

CHAPTER VI

EVALUATION

Evaluation is one of the most important and one of the most often ignored components in any educational program. Its importance in bilingual programs is perhaps even greater because of their innovative qualities. Although there are sound bases in existing educational and psychological research reports to assure us that bilingualism is advantageous, there are many questions still to be answered about using two languages in school. What teaching techniques will prove most successful in different situations? How will the program design affect long-range achievement? Which instructional materials are best suited for which groups of children? What degree of interaction should there be with relevant culturally oriented activities? Even our evaluation instruments themselves need to be assessed.

With the rapidly expanding scope of bilingual education in the United States today, we can soon have a wealth of information in answer to these and other pertinent questions. This will allow future bilingual programs, and existing programs in future years, to build on past experiences, improve and refine instructional design, techniques, and materials, and greatly increase the success potential of students from linguistically different backgrounds. We will have this information, however, only if innovative bilingual projects report on their procedures and progress in a way that allows objective evaluation and comparative assessment among programs.

Many roadblocks lie in the way of reliable analysis, including the lack of completely appropriate evaluation measures, but we can make the best use of what is available now and participate in the development of better instruments.

No single achievement test for students at the end of the year will indicate what has been going on in their classrooms. We need to know where they started when they entered that classroom, what cultural conditions were affecting their achievement, and what their capacity for learning is. This requires at least an achievement test at the beginning and end of the year (a pretest and posttest), a brief description of the students' home environment, and a test of intelligence. The pretesting is absolutely essential to gain baseline data against which to measure pupil progress and program effectiveness.

Language tests

The most important area to test for in the fall and spring is competence in both languages of instruction. It is important not to jump to the conclusion that a child doesn't have control over any language just because he is not willing to talk or even respond to questions or directions at the beginning of the school year. Some children choose not to talk so early in the program, and others are too shy to. An unfamiliar person in the classroom may intimidate a child, who may in turn take refuge in not speaking or using minimal replies. Care should be taken that ratings of verbal fluency not be taken on the basis of interview situations such as this.

More sophisticated tests of language capacity should include measurement of both recognition and production of the sound system, common grammatical elements, and a representative lexicon in both languages. Any evaluation measure used with young children must be short, require little ability to follow directions, and little skill requiring marking pictures or following items in sequence. Ideally, the measure should be administered by the teacher or aide rather than by a stranger in the classroom. In addition, it should be immediately usable by the teacher in evaluating the children's progress and making appropriate adjustment in grouping and rate of instruction, and yet contain in the responses enough additional data for whatever more detailed linguistic analysis is desired at a later time. The test should also be a standardized measure which could later be replicated with other groups of children if comparative data is desired. Unfortunately, no such ideal test has yet been developed. Adequate measures are available, however, or may be constructed by the staff or a consulting linguist.

The kind of item which tests for the recognition of sound in the language is a pair of pictures whose labels differ only in the one sound being tested—a minimal pair, such as mouse and mouth, or ship and sheep. The children are then told to mark (or put their finger on) the mouth, the ship, and one picture of each pair presented. Lexicon can be tested in a similar fashion with children asked to mark a picture which represents the word named by the tester. It is more difficult to picture grammatical structures, but pictures can be prepared to illustrate differences between the rabbit which is painting and the rabbit which is painted, the boy who has a cold and the boy who is cold, the dog which is going to eat and the dog which has eaten, and similar constructions.

The production of sounds and of vocabulary items can be tested at the same time by asking children to name pictures or objects. The numbers one to ten and the names of the colors of crayons in a crayon box will provide a fast preliminary screening of each child's production of some of the sounds of each language. However, a properly-constructed test should contain all of the phonemes in the language, and should sample the phonemes in different relevant positions in the word (initially, medially, finally, and in various clusters). This speech sample should be taped so the teacher can record the errors quickly, and so that the record can be compared with the child's pronunciation at the end of the year. (The teacher may enlist the help of a speech therapist or other person in the school with more training in listening for speech sounds.) A child's ability to use sentences in any language can be quickly tested by asking him to describe a few pictures in that language or to tell a story. His responses should be tape-recorded and used as a rough measure of progress at a later date. Such initial screening devices do not take the place of a professional testing program to ascertain the children's linguistic competencies. They are only meant to provide a "first aid" measure for the teacher who needs to have some immediate information in order to begin teaching.

A few standardized tests can be adapted to testing for language competence, even though that is not their stated purpose. The Metropolitan Reading Readiness test section on word meaning provides some measure of English usage, and the Murphy-Durrell Reading Readiness Analysis section on phoneme identification will also provide interesting and useful information. The Habilidad-General contains a vocabulary section of both English and Spanish forms which could be used as a rough measure of growth in each language or to help determine which is the child's dominant language, or his degree of bilingualism. An individual production test, the Peabody Picture Vocabulary test, has recently been translated into Spanish and its two forms may be used for the same purposes. The responses to this can and should also be tape-recorded.

Two very promising approaches to testing for language development are: 1) oral repetition of model sentences, and 2) judging grammaticality of presented word sequences. The oral repetition procedure allows the tester to control precisely for children's mastery of particular points of phonology, grammar, or sentence length. The only presently available test of this type is based on the Gloria and David materials, which provides for tape recording of the child's responses. The second type of test, though less reliable, shows that as children grow older, they are able to make finer and finer distinctions regarding the ungrammaticality or grammaticality of certain word sequences (e.g. Went to town he vs. He like the book). Unfortunately, no test of this type is currently available.

Standardized tests of achievement are available for subjects conducted in English from the first grade up, but none are yet adequate for testing achievement in bilingual programs. Particular care must be taken not to judge the achievement of children in bilingual programs against monolingual norms in the early stages of instruction. Since the first year of reading should be taught in the dominant language of each child, it is particularly pointless to test reading achievement in English only and draw any conclusions from the results.

Home conditions

Because student achievement is often vitally affected by such factors as numbers of brothers and sisters, ordinal rank in family, and educational level and occupation of parents, it is important that information on these factors be obtained for each child. It is also important to know the sociolinguistic makeup of the home: what languages are spoken there, for what purpose, by whom, and what attitudes are expressed toward each language and their speakers. In addition, the place of origin of the parents may figure significantly, since a child whose parents are recent immigrants from Mexico or Puerto Rico may be very differently circumstanced, and have a different cultural background, from one whose parents are natives of the area. Also, such matters as whether the child's parents are employed at a stable occupation or are migrant workers can be very significant.

The following interview form has been used by cooperative educational research projects and provides a handy form for recording valuable information. The rating of the child's use of Spanish and English is meant to be the family's opinion of his language fluency. The rating of the housing is completed by the interviewer after the interview is finished.

HOME INTERVIEW

Name of student _____
Teacher _____ Class _____
Sex _____ Birthdate _____ Birthplace _____
Father's birthplace _____ Mother's birthplace _____
No. of children _____ Ordinal rank _____
Entered _____ Left _____ Days present _____

CHILD'S USE OF SPANISH
_____ (1) Little or no facility in Spanish.
_____ (2) Able to understand simple directions but unable to carry on a conversation.

___ (3) Able to carry on a conversation.

CHILD'S USE OF ENGLISH
___ (1) Little or no facility in English.
___ (2) Able to understand simple directions but unable to carry on a conversation.
___ (3) Able to carry on a conversation.

HOUSING
___ (1) Shack or substandard house in slum area.
___ (2) Deteriorating area with marginal housing.
___ (3) Home in average residential area of well-kept property, neat but of moderate cost.
___ (4) Better than average homes or apartments but short of luxury.
___ (5) Private, large, well-kept home or "luxury" apartment in preferred residential area.

HOME LANGUAGE
___ (1) Both parents use Spanish almost exclusively with children.
___ (2) One parent uses Spanish and the other uses English with children.
___ (3) Both parents use Spanish and English more than casually with children.
___ (4) Both parents use English almost exclusively with children.

EDUCATION OF THE HEAD OF FAMILY OR THE PARENT WHO SEEMS TO INFLUENCE MOST THE STATUS OF THE FAMILY
___ (1) Completed less than 8 years of elementary school.
___ (2) Completed 8th grade but less than senior high school.
___ (3) Completed senior high school.
___ (4) Completed a year or more of college work.
___ (5) Attended graduate or professional school at least one year.

OCCUPATION OF PARENT PROVIDING MOST SUPPORT
___ (1) Unemployed (not retired), on relief, odd jobs only, work giving very low wages, etc.
___ (2) Low income but regular work, waiters, farm laborers, semi-skilled work, etc.
___ (3) Skilled labor, carpenter, police, fireman, small business, electrician, small landowner, salesman, foreman, etc.
___ (4) Teachers, librarians, smaller businesses, managers, supervisors, registered nurse, etc.
___ (5) Professions and high-income occupations: lawyer, physician, engineer, college professor, school administrator, large business proprietor or large landowner, executive in corporation or bank, editor, CPA, etc.

Intelligence tests

Some measure of the children's IQ will also be desired, but this can be delayed until later in the school year. No verbal measure of intelligence has been found to be reliable with children who have linguistically different backgrounds. Using such tests for the assignment of children to classrooms in a controlled research design is even questionable in the primary grades. A random assignment of students to the experimental classrooms is probably as likely to equalize the groups when all children come from the same general background as any tests which might be given. In fact, such variables as expectancy factors when IQ scores are assigned make it seem likely that testing intelligence at the beginning of the program might even have negative effects. When an IQ test is administered, the Goodenough-Harris Draw-a-Man test is proving quite satisfactory in terms of ease in administration and correlation with other standardized tests of intelligence. Some individual tests of intelligence (such as the Stanford-Binet) have been translated into other languages and can be given to a random sample as time and funds permit.

One of the hazards to objective testing is the teacher's unconscious desire to help the children, or see them do better on the tests. Another is variable scoring procedure among different individuals. If the Goodenough-Harris is selected as an intelligence measure, an excellent manual is available with complete scoring instructions. The scoring is time consuming, and should not be required of the classroom teachers. If more than one person is scoring the pictures, a random sample (such as one in every ten) should be cross-checked for consistency. Individual intelligence tests such as the Stanford-Binet or WISC require extensive training for proper administration and interpretation. Time and money factors may therefore make their use with all students impossible, but they may be used with only a random sample of the population as a means of validating other data. That is to say, if the IQ scores obtained for a random sample of the children (e.g., every tenth child) on the Stanford-Binet correlate closely with the IQ scores secured for the same children on a less time-consuming test (which was given to the whole group), then more faith may be placed in the validity of the group test.

Testing hints

Evaluation is a necessary component of educational programs, but teachers can quite understandably lose sight of some of its value if they face disrupted schedules and unhappy children. Administrators and teachers can help prevent problems (and unreliable test results) by following these suggestions:

schedule pretesting the first month of school, but not during the first week. Children and teachers need a chance to get settled a little.
if tests contain such directives as "draw a circle around ____" or "make an X on ____," teach the directions a day ahead of time with material not included in the tests.
keep testing periods short. At the beginning of school, the children should not be expected to sit still for more than twenty minutes at a time.
test in small groups or have an assistant present for every ten children. It is necessary to check constantly at this level to see if everyone is in the right place, and even to see if all the booklets are right side up. One teacher checking twenty-five children loses the attention of the class.
keep the atmosphere relaxed and happy.
follow the stated testing procedure exactly.

A great deal of work still remains to be done in the construction and validation of tests of bilingual education programs. As such tests are being developed and made available, necessary checks on the progress of children and programs is going to come from the combined observation of experienced and knowledgeable teachers, coordinators, administrators, and linguists.

SELECTED BIBLIOGRAPHY

Fishman, Joshua A. 1967. The measurement and description of language dominance in bilinguals. Final report, phase 1. ERIC No. ED 016 954.
Harris, David P. 1969. Testing English as a second language. New York, McGraw-Hill.
Hopkins, Thomas R. 1967. Language testing of North American Indians. Washington, D.C., Department of the Interior, Bureau of Indian Affairs.
Kelly, L. G., ed. 1969. Description and measurement of bilingualism. Toronto, Canada, The University of Toronto Press.
Kittell, J. 1963. Intelligence-test performance of children from bilingual environments. Elementary school journal LXIV, 2, Nov., 76-83.
Lado, Robert. 1964. Language testing. New York, McGraw-Hill.
Manuel, Herschel T. 1966. Development of inter-American test materials. Austin, The University of Texas.
Spolsky, Bernard. 1968. Language testing; the problem of validation. TESOL quarterly, June, 88-94. ERIC No. ED 023 077.

Do Not Remove __8/08__ Date

LC
3715
.S2
1975

43651

Saville, Muriel R.
  A Handbook of Bilingual
Education.

St. Joseph's College Library
Brentwood, New York